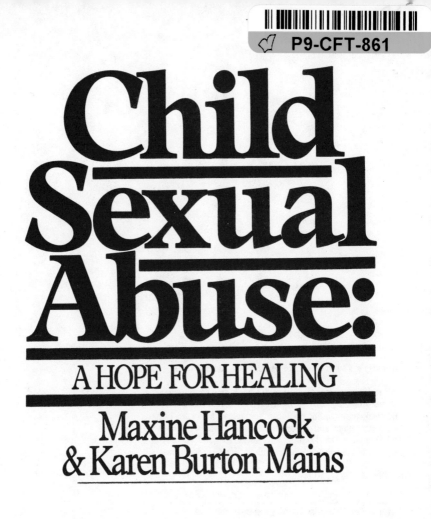

Child Sexual Abuse:

A HOPE FOR HEALING

Maxine Hancock
& Karen Burton Mains

Harold Shaw Publishers
Wheaton, Illinois

ISBN 0–87788–150–2

Library of Congress Cataloging-in-Publication Data
Hancock, Maxine.
    Child sexual abuse.

    Bibliography: p.
    Includes index.
    1. Child molesting—United States.   2. Adult
child abuse victims—United States.   3. Child
molesting—Religious aspects—Christianity.
I. Mains, Karen Burton.   II. Title.
HQ72.U53H34   1987   362.7'044   86-26284
ISBN 0-87788-150-2

---

96   95   94   93   92   91   90   89
10   9   8   7   6   5   4

Contents

Acknowledgments

Karen and I have taken a pilgrimage to painful awareness in the process of writing this book. But we have not traveled alone. Our special thanks go to the many survivors to whom we talked, and especially to the four who shared so wholly their stories of deep pain and healing: Kathy, Rita, George, and Margaret. The names are, of course, invented. Some details are slightly altered to protect the identities of the storytellers. But these Voices—and all those in this book—are the authentic voices of child sexual abuse survivors.

We have frequently sought expert opinion, and we express our thanks especially to Helen Hewitt, Director of the Sexual Assault Center in Lloydminster, Canada, and to Dr. J. E. Runions, Medical Director of the British Columbia Hospital in Coquitlam for reviewing early drafts of the manuscript and making valuable observations, and to the directors of the many assault centers we contacted. We are thankful to all who have participated in this book by allowing us to use the articles and books on child abuse that are included in the notes and bibliography.

Most especially, we thank Harold and Luci Shaw who caught the vision of this book and its ministry and held it before us when we faltered. Harold Shaw, who died before seeing the manuscript completed, believed with us that lives could be made new through a knowledge and application of the truth of God's Word. Our many thanks to Luci Shaw for her encouragement and love and to Luci and Ramona Tucker for their editing expertise.

To all, our thanks.

Maxine Hancock

Introduction

" 'Woman, why are you weeping?'

These words of the risen Lord to Mary Magdalene are some of the most powerful ever spoken to a woman by a man . . ."

With these words, I began a three-week series on the topic *Abuse: What Can We Do?* for our national daily radio broadcast *The Chapel of the Air.* Though I knew the problem was widespread, I was not prepared for the enormous response from men and women across the country.

Nor was I prepared for a phone message on my desk indicating that Maxine Hancock had called: Was I planning a book on the topic? She, too, had planned such a project, but could she leave it to me, if I was also doing one?

I certainly wasn't! After spending six months in intensive research on the topic of abuse, three weeks on actual broadcasting, and reading and answering hundreds of letters from listeners who had been victims of abuse, I was weary of walking around this rim of vicarious suffering and eager to move on to less distressing projects.

Then I stopped to listen to that insistent inner word spoken to me in another tone of voice, "Woman, why are you weeping?—don't weep. Work!"; I changed my selfish heart, called Maxine, and suggested that we pray about co-authoring a book on this urgent topic.

Maxine, like myself, a writer and conference speaker, has addressed all kinds of women's groups in a variety of church denominations. As itinerant ministers we have both discovered that we are like visiting priests. People confess burdens they feel they cannot share with those in their familiar everyday lives. We've had women tell us things they've never told their own husbands. All too many have said to us, "I couldn't tell this to my pastor. I don't think he'd understand." And more women than I can count have explained, "I don't have anyone I can talk to about this. They wouldn't believe me."

Maxine and I have heard countless stories of early child sexual abuse. We have ministered and counseled with men and women who were struggling with the long-range effects of this aberration. We both have intimate friendships with those who have undergone years of pain from incestuous pasts but who through God's grace are now facing the truth, moving toward the light, and growing whole, emotionally and psychologically; brave and courageous souls who amaze us with their capacity to function even within their painful context as godly men and women, as healers, as nurturers.

Given this unique exposure and understanding, how could we possibly refuse to speak for those who could not speak for themselves? How could we dare look away from the pain? As neither Maxine nor I have experienced child abuse first-hand, we have a consequent objectivity (if not a holy obligation) to reveal, to explain, to comfort, to encourage, to be agents for healing. In addition, between the two of us, our resources were vast; the Voices of actual survivors who had shared with us their pain, lived in our homes for awhile, and been our friends and confidantes could speak for themselves through our writing. Maxine and I began to see how we could be conduits through which these Voices of early child sexual abuse could speak. They verify our reporting of statistics and studies with personal testimony and experience.

Without experiencing it first-hand, we have gone through much of the trauma of this abuse: we have felt the shock, disbelief, and repugnance; we have spent nights in tears at the magnitude of this kind of violation of God's plan. But we have also sensed the privilege of sharing in this fellowship of suffering and developed an inner toughness —a determination to take a hard look at the pain and do something.

Maxine has truly borne much of the book's research and organization; and when one of us grew soul-sick during the writing process, she would turn over the work to the other. This has been a joint effort so solid that our plural voice *we* comfortably becomes *I* in the body of the book. Living half a continent away from each other, we have nevertheless been of one mind and heart, often hearing in prayer similar guidelines from God that made the work go well. We consider this to be God's book and a labor of love completed with a feeling of positive joy because, although we have heard the stories of pain, we are also overwhelmed by the incredible possibilities for healing.

I am convinced that this book can be a tool of liberation, that it will bring comfort, encourage the healing process to begin, and inject a faltering belief system with doses of hope. These chapters are not only designed for survivors of early child sexual abuse but are also to be used by helpers who compassionately seek to understand. It is time to join holy hands and lift holy prayers against sexual practices which may seem modern and "liberated" to some but have evil derivations as ancient as the fertility rites of those who once worshipped at the phallic altars of Baal and Ashteroth.

We pray that as you read you will begin not only to know about the power of a God who is truly greater than other gods but that you will experience his tender love, his gentle acceptance, his awesome ability to pour grace into the most damaged of hearts and minds. It is a love and power that brings order, dignity, and purpose out of blackest chaos.

Through all our reading and listening, Maxine and I have become convinced that women who suffered child sexual abuse need advocates—many of them—and that the church is the social institution best equipped to bring healing. We also believe that it is the male Christ who is a woman's greatest Advocate, Healer, and Sympathizer.

We feel compelled to insist with the Voices who have so eloquently spoken that it is Christ who stood beside the death tomb long ago and spoke gently to an anguished woman, and it is he who still stands beside the weeping women of this generation in the mourning places of their own lives. He still asks, with deepest concern, "Woman, why are you weeping?"

It is Christ who is present (if we will only learn to recognize him) at the death scenes of our pasts. It is he who heals the memories. It is he who rolls away the gravestones which seal in all the decaying carnage of our human degradation. And it is he who speaks our names so we can look up and see that the garden-green resurrection day is dawning.

Our prayer is that you will meet him, one by one, and that he will make you whole.

Karen Mains

Kathy

Kathy is a professional woman with a wide range of abilities. Besides being trained as a psychiatric nurse, she skillfully manages her home. A loving wife and mother, Kathy experienced both the pain of sexual abuse and the joy of healing. She shares her story with us.

1
The Nature of
Child Sexual Abuse

Kathy's Story:

My childhood was very normal until I was about five years of age. Beginning at the age of five and continuing until I was almost twelve, I was sexually abused by an uncle who lived close by, who was almost like a big brother to me. He was nineteen when it started. I trusted him then; it was fun to be with him. He used to take me around with him—a very big deal to a five-year-old.

All of this developed gradually. He started taking me to the barn to be alone with him. Later, he began to fondle me and expose himself to me, and ask me to kiss and handle him. I knew within myself that this wasn't right, but he kept telling me that this was our secret and that I wasn't ever to tell anybody. He promised he would never hurt me. It is true that he was never violent or angry. It was always "in love," so to speak.

Even though I knew it was somehow wrong, I was afraid to say anything or to go to anybody about it. But as years went on, his handling of me became more and more aggressive.

At some point during those years, I attempted to tell my mother. I don't really remember what I said, but I was not able to make her understand. She knew I had grown to dislike this particular uncle. She may have denied the reason, or perhaps I failed to communicate the reality to her. Anyhow, it became a closed door between us.

The abuse finally stopped when my family moved away from the farm and I no longer had any contact with my uncle. When we made a return visit a year or so later, he again tried to attack me. But I was able to resist. I was old enough then and very afraid. I realized that I did have some rights.

It's strange, isn't it? As a child you feel like you don't have any right to question what an adult is doing. You are brought up to respect adults and think that they know what is best. I found myself saying, "Well, I guess it must be O.K. . . . He's a grown-up."

* ✳ *

Child sexual abuse. Finally we have a name for the unspeakable, the unthinkable. For too long, survivors of child sexual abuse have lived in a suffocating darkness of silence. There were no words with which to name their wounds; no ears to hear their cries.

Now at last we are hearing their stories. Their pain is reaching out and touching our own nerves. Kathy's true story, which we will follow from abuse to recovery, is typical. She is one of thousands of women who must be heard. We will begin to hear their Voices in this book and then, if we listen, we will begin to recognize them all around us.

I didn't realize the extent of abuse in America—I have felt so alone with this problem . . .

* ✳ *

When my sisters and I were growing up, sexually abused by our stepfather, we didn't realize that we were a few statistic points in a large and growing population . . .

* ✳ *

Some years ago, memories I thought were buried surfaced anew. About this same time the media began to explore and report on the subject of incest. Would you believe it was not until then that I really knew what the word meant and that I was a victim?

Despite the overwhelming evidence that child sexual abuse may still be an under-reported crime, we all must fight a strong desire to deny or avoid this subject. Survivors wish they could forget about it but know that they cannot. Most of those who have not felt the pain simply prefer not to deal with information about child sexual abuse.

Moving from ignorance to awareness is a costly step. After a meeting in which I had spoken about child sexual abuse, a young woman came to talk with me, identifying herself as an incest survivor. "I almost didn't come tonight," she said. "When anything about incest comes on the television, I switch channels or get out of the room. It's just too painful. But now I know I have to face my past." I can understand her struggle with avoidance, even denial. As I have researched this subject, I have gone through an emotional progression from shock and horror to terrible anger and then into deep grief. Finally, out of that grief has come the determination to speak and to act.

What Constitutes Child Sexual Abuse?
I should have sought help sooner, but in my ignorance as to what constitutes abuse, I never saw it as such and so was unaware of the root of my misery . . .

Many survivors ask, "Was I abused? Am I a victim?" They are not alone in being unsure as to what constitutes sexual abuse. Even professional sources don't agree on the specific definitions regarding child sexual abuse.

Let's spell it out.

Child sexual abuse covers a broad range of sexually-oriented activities which involve the child. These range from sexual exposure and fondling all the way to anal or vaginal penetration. The following activities are considered to be sexually abusive:

—an adult showing a child his/her genitals
—an adult asking a child to undress to be looked at or fondled

5

—an adult touching a child's genitals
—an adult having a child touch his/her genitals
—oral-genital contact
—forced masturbation
—digital penetration, or penetration of anus or vagina with another object
—anal penetration
—intercourse
—use of children for the production of pornographic materials

Sexual abuse of children consists of activities which expose children to sexual stimulation inappropriate to their age, psychological development, and role in the family.

When such activities occur between family members, the term *incest* or *intrafamilial child sexual abuse* is applied. Alexander G. Zaphiris broadly defines incest as sexual activity on the part of an adult "related either by blood or by legal action, or . . . through social channels (for example, the incestuous adult may be a neighbor or a tenant in the child's family dwelling). In the latter case, the social relationship has been long-standing so that the adult has achieved a status of authority."[1]

Most researchers apply the term *incest* somewhat more exclusively than Zaphiris but still include not only blood relatives but also adults who live in a family relationship to the child: stepfathers, stepbrothers, stepgrandparents. Figure 1.1 shows the various approaches to defining incest.

Child sexual abuse which is perpetrated by someone outside of the family—a babysitter, family friend, or unknown molester, is termed *extrafamilial child sexual abuse*.

Do these things really happen? Hear a few of the Voices I have heard:

As a small child my father initiated "secret" meetings with me. He touched me in places I felt were wrong, but he said it was a "game." He also made me touch him in places I didn't like. As time went on I realized I enjoyed the feeling despite the guilt . . . I have lived with enormous guilt because I was willing to take part in this sin.

Definitions of Incest

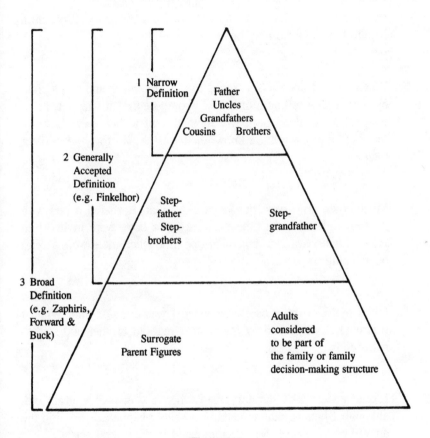

Figure 1.1

Various definitions of the term *incest* exist in research literature. Narrowly used, the term refers to sexual activities between blood-relatives. Broadly used, it includes sexual activities initiated by any adult who plays the role of a family member in the life of the child. The broader definition is becoming generally accepted.

I don't know if I am truly a "victim."

* * *

About the time I was thirteen or fourteen, my dad would come into my bedroom and proceed to "pet" me and make me "pet" him. Night after night I'd pray he wouldn't . . .

* * *

When I was fifteen, I was raped by my stepfather and had a child by him. I kept telling him it was wrong; he said it was not, as he was not a blood relation. My mother went to her grave blaming me, but he ought to have known better as he was forty years older than I . . .

* * *

My brother, who was four years older than I, shared a bed with me. Enough said? As time went on other boys were invited into "fun" situations. I can remember one time when there were several boys taking turns . . .

* * *

I was molested by a babysitter when I was three or four. When I was nine, I was raped by my sixteen-year-old brother and sold to his friends . . .

* * *

I was a victim of statutory rape when I was twelve years old, although I believe that something probably happened to me in the area of abuse long before it culminated in the sexual act . . .

* * *

As a little girl I was a victim of sexual fondling by a much older cousin. Though this cousin used all of his younger girl cousins in this way, our families did nothing but tell us to keep away from him . . .

* ✳ *

I was sexually stimulated as a baby so very early in life that I craved sexual stimulation. . .

* ✳ *

My first sexual experience was at age four . . .

* ✳ *

I was sexually abused by my father from the time when I was a very tiny child until I began dating . . . I was brought up to obey my parents and felt there must be something wrong with me. My younger sister also recently confessed to being sexually abused . . .

The real horror of these stories is that the great majority of those who are sexually abused experience the abuse from someone they know and trust. And unlike sexual molestation, which is often a sudden and forceful event, intrafamilial child sexual abuse is usually continued over a long period of time. The child's trust has been gained only to be betrayed. Sexual activity often begins with a subtle progression from normal loving touch to sexual fondling. The child, naturally confused, often accepts the authority of the adult as warrant that the activity is either all right or unavoidable. Sandra Butler writes:

> Needs for human contact and warmth become translated into the specific sexual form of [a] father's stroking and fondling. In a home in which the only love and tenderness a girl receives takes the form of sexual play, the child's slowly growing sense of the wrongness of such intimacy takes years to surface and, when it does, is coupled with her own incorporated feelings of guilt and responsibility for having let it go on.[2]

Kathy's story illustrates very clearly what Zaphiris calls "the conditioning phrase" in which the child is gradually conditioned to accept an adult's sexual behavior as "part and parcel of love and affection."[3]

How Common is Child Sexual Abuse?

"Living in a small rural community," a police officer states, "I am aware that many of our citizens choose to believe that child abuse couldn't or doesn't happen here. It is this kind of thinking that allows child abuse to flourish."

How many people are affected by child sexual abuse? The evidence keeps coming in, each study presenting higher percentages of the population reporting child sexual abuse. Early reporting represented only the tip of the iceberg.

Children tend to keep their sexual abuse experiences secret (for reasons discussed in Chapter 2, Figure 2.2). Therefore, most knowledge about the incidence of child sexual abuse must be gained from adults recalling experiences which occurred in their childhoods. Obviously, there are some difficulties with accuracy and detail with this form of reporting; but based on recall, researchers discovered that one in five to one in three of the females surveyed reported they had experienced undesired sexual activity as children.

Since Russell's study (Figure 1.2) was based on a sociometrically accurate random sample of adult women and an extensive interview-type questionnaire, it would seem to be the most complete study to date. Looking at her conclusions a bit more closely, we find the following:

Two Landmark Studies of Incidence[4]

Date	Researcher	Sample	Percentage of Sample Reporting Sexual Abuse Before Age of 18	
			Extrafamilial	Intrafamilial
1978	David Finkelhor	530 females	19%	14%
1983	Diana Russell	930 randomly selected women in San Francisco	31%	16%

Figure 1.2

10

—16% of the 930 women surveyed reported at least one experience of intrafamilial sexual abuse before the age of eighteen.

—12% of these women had been sexually abused by a relative before the age of fourteen.

—When intrafamilial and extrafamilial categories of child sexual abuse are combined, 38% of the 930 women reported at least one experience of intrafamilial and/or extrafamilial sexual abuse before the age of eighteen. 28% reported at least one such experience before the age of fourteen.

It is important to note that these rates of incidence are based on definitions of sexual abuse which exclude such non-contact experiences as exhibitionism or sexual advances not acted upon. When these kinds of experiences are included, the number of women with such an experience before age eighteen goes up to 54 percent, with 48 percent having had such an experience before age fourteen. The researcher comments: "While these prevalence figures for child sexual abuse are shockingly high, it would be interesting to know how much higher they would be had broader definitions of both intrafamilial and extrafamilial child sexual abuse more comparable to some other studies been adopted."[5]

Who Are the Perpetrators of Child Sexual Abuse?

—Fathers. Stepfathers. Uncles. Brothers. Cousins.

—Trusted family friends.

—The nice man next door.

In at least 75 percent of child sexual abuse cases the perpetrator is someone the child loves and knows. (Most recent figures push this figure closer to 95 percent.) Figure 1.3 shows what is known about sexual abusers.

Sick, sordid, unspeakably selfish, the perpetrators of child sexual abuse exploit the innocence and trust of young children for their own sexual gratification. We will take a closer look at the perpetrator in chapter eleven.

But Not in the Church, Surely?

Sadly, we have to concur with the mounting evidence that child sexual abuse also occurs within church-oriented homes. Being in a family that is "religious," even "evangelical" or "fundamental," does not guarantee a youngster protection from sexual abuse. In fact, studies indicate that child sexual abuse occurs at almost the same rate of incidence in all levels of society.

Dr. Richard Butman, clinical psychologist and associate professor of psychology at Wheaton College, writes:

> Despite the clear prohibition of incest in Leviticus 6-18, the majority of reported aggressors are regular church attenders. It is difficult to measure someone's "Christianity," but researchers do report that the adult males tend to be very devout, moralistic, and conservative in their religious beliefs . . . [7]

Perpetrator Characteristics: Summary from Sexual Abuse Reports[6]

	1976-1982 Composite: Sexual Abuse Reports	Comments
Perpetrator Characteristics		
Average Age (years)	35.3	
Sex		
—Percentage Male	79.0	Most perpetrators of sexual abuse are male.
—Percentage Female	21.0	
Relationship to Involved Children		
—Percentage Parent	77.4	Nearly 94% of perpetrators are related to the abused child.
—Percentage Other Relatives	16.3	
—Percentage Other	6.3	

Figure 1.3

The Voices I have been listening to speak from within the church as well as from the wider community:

> I am sixty-one years old, but when I was grade school aged I was molested by a family adult who was a young minister of about twenty-two years of age.

* ❋ *

> Having been sexually abused by my father—in a so-called "Christian" home—for a period of approximately seven years, you can imagine some of the difficulty and confusion that I've experienced throughout my life (I am forty-three years old now).

* ❋ *

> Are there any normal Christian families? When my two oldest girls were in their teens, their grandfather, a faithful church member, was putting his hands where they never should be. He showed the girls pornographic material. He paid another girl to let him "feel." He remains in everyone's memory as a "great pillar of the Church."

* ❋ *

> After telling of incestuous experiences as a child, a woman says, "I should add that my father is a Christian and I was raised in a good evangelical church which we attended faithfully."

The problem exists. Because we want it to go away does not mean that it will go away. Our very silence allows it to grow to horrifying proportions. Abused children all too frequently become adults who abuse their own children. The sins of the father are being visited upon the children. Silence will not help survivors pick up the pieces of long-term sexual problems, wretched self-images, or severe personality disorders. Nor will silence confront the guilty with their need of confession, forgiveness, and redemption. Two things need to be broken—first our long, uneasy silence; then, as a consequence, the cycle of sexual abuse.

The Church, empowered by the living Christ, is able to offer healing through supportive, loving community only when we lose our fear of walking into the hell of pain-filled lives so that the abused as well as the abuser can be set free.

This is our assignment.

To hear each others' stories. To feel each others' pain. With divine power to set each other free.

So help us, God.

2

The Physical
and Emotional
Aftermath

Kathy's Story:

As I got a little older—after I was ten or so—I thought a lot about what my uncle and I did together. The sexual activity seemed to have developed into a need within me. It became something I hated and yet something that, in spite of myself, I almost looked forward to. In time, I felt I was as much responsible for what was happening as he was. I had a lot of inner guilt because a part of me enjoyed the stimulation.

I felt that I was different from other children, living in a world of my own. I felt like I had never really been a child. It seemed I had been plunged into an adult world and I never did the normal things that kids around me did. Naturally I wondered: What is different about me? Why does he do this to me? Is there something wrong with me that makes him choose me?

When my parents moved and the whole affair came to a sudden stop, I developed an intense hatred for my uncle. I felt that he had ruined my life, leaving me nothing worth living for. Many, many times I thought about how I might kill him. I thought that if I could just get him off the face of the earth, maybe I could forget about the whole thing.

Throughout my teenage years, I was suicidal. If I couldn't get rid of him, I felt the next best thing was to get rid of myself. I thought about killing myself many times and actually attempted suicide when I was seventeen. I took an overdose of sleeping pills and ended up in the hospital for a couple of weeks. That only made me feel worse about myself.

Having been exposed to sex at such an early age, I had intense sexual struggles. The drives that were a part of normal adolescence were, for me, explosive, creating tremendous conflict for me. I dated a lot during my teens, using dating situations as a way to get back at men. I had no respect for males. Period. I knew you couldn't trust them, knew they were only looking for one thing, knew they were users. So I used them and abused them. For me, dating was a chance to play a game of torment, arousing my partner as much as possible and then rebuffing him short of going all the way. At the same time, of course, I was tormenting myself.

Meanwhile I managed to maintain my studies. I made good grades in school and went into nursing, hoping that I would discover something that would help me understand how to overcome what I was struggling with. The courses I enjoyed most were psychology and sociology; but although I studied them intensely and read everything I could find in the library, I still couldn't find anything that could help me.

Increasingly, life became a struggle. I wanted to live just one day of my life without thinking about my past or without having it affect me. That's all I wanted—one day without flashbacks or horrible memories, just one day without anger and hatred consuming me.

The whole thing seemed too horrible to tell anybody. I wanted to talk with someone many times. But then I would think, "It all happened so long ago—what's the point of saying anything about it now?" Even when a psychiatrist talked with me after my attempted suicide, I wouldn't tell him the whole story.

I was nearly twenty-six before I met a man I felt I could actually trust, a very kind and loving man. Despite my emotional problems during nursing training, I had achieved my professional goals and was an established and respected psychiatric nurse. I longed for a home and family, but although I knew I really cared for this man, I was very afraid of marriage, uncertain as to whether I was capable of loving a man with constancy. So I literally entered marriage with a clearly defined escape clause. If it didn't work, I decided, I would just have to get a divorce.

At first our sexual relationship was difficult—very guarded, very tense. Much as I cared for my husband, I still found the physical relationship difficult. Frequently, flashbacks interfered. I began to think that if I didn't change in my response to him, I would lose him. So with grit and determination, I literally exerted mind over matter, determined to overcome that problem.

We had some happy years; the birth of our first son thrilled us, and I was very much wrapped up in this new life. Although I was still struggling daily, I was coping. Anyone looking at me from the outside would not have guessed that I was having difficulty. Even my husband had no idea of the past that still shadowed me.

* ✳ *

Kathy's story illustrates many of the most commonly reported long-term struggles of child sexual abuse victims. The word "survivor" is an apt description for those who live with an abusive past. Like survivors of other life changing traumas, many carry scars inflicted on them by the actions of other people for the rest of their lives.

We need to listen closely to the Voices of these survivors and begin to map out what psychotherapist Susan Forward calls "the emotional geography of incest."[1] Such a map can, in turn, help abuse survivors identify characteristics of the terrain they traverse in their own pilgrimage toward wholeness and recovery.

Because my sources, and those reporting to other researchers, are nearly all women, I will speak of survivors in the feminine gender. However, the dynamics which operate so disruptively apply to male victims of child sexual abuse as well. (There is a growing sense among

17

researchers that sexual abuse of male children is very much under-reported and that the ratio of male to female victims may be as high as four to six.)

There are, of course, dissenting voices within society that pose the question, "What's wrong with adult/child sex?" Some organized groups lobby to promote pedophilia as a lifestyle. (A pedophile is someone, usually male, who has a strong sexual interest in children.) Such groups as the North American Man/Boy Love Association (NAMBLA) urge that the age of consent should be lowered to four years of age.

The notorious René Guyon Society, based in southern California, has a motto of "Sex before age eight, or else it's too late." The Childhood Sensuality Circle (CSC), based in San Diego, California, has a nine-point statement of purpose concerning the sexual rights of children. While these groups are small in membership, they are active in lobbying at state and federal levels for changes in laws relating to children and sex. For those of us who have worked with and listened to survivors of incest and other forms of child sexual abuse, the possibility that serious attention is being given to ideas which would strip children of even the very minimal existing legal protection that they have can only evoke horror.

Ask Somebody Who Has Been Through It

In *Kiss Daddy Goodnight*, Louise Armstrong reports on her own and others' experiences of incest. Her answer to the question, "What's wrong with it?" is frank and blunt: "Oh, god. Tell them to ask somebody who's been through it."[2]

As Florence Rush states in *The Best Kept Secret*, "Once we perceive, question, and challenge the existence of the sexual abuse of children, we have taken the first crucial step toward the elimination of the degradation, humiliation, and corrosion of our most valuable human resource—our young."[3]

It is, of course, difficult to establish absolute cause-and-effect relationships between child sexual abuse and the many problems which survivors experience and attribute to it. "I know I blamed everything that happened to me, *everything*, on the incest in my childhood," a young woman told me. Some researchers have noted that child sexual abuse becomes a central focus around which negative experiences and emotions cluster.[4] But there is overwhelming evidence that a childhood sexual experience with an older person is negative and damaging, with "long-range effects on the quality of personal adjustments and interpersonal relationships."[5] The aftereffects may vary in intensity and severity, but they are common to most who have experienced child sexual abuse.

As examples of the personal pain and turmoil which may exist even in those who seem to have made an adequate adjustment to life, Steele and Alexander list the following:

—feelings of inferiority
—non-integrated personality
—poor basic trust
—repressed anger
—unresolved identifications and fixations
—difficulties in establishing and maintaining relationships
—sexual dysfunction and/or aberrant sexual behaviors
—shame, guilt, and fear of social disapproval
—underlying feelings of helplessness and fear[6]

Such a litany of pain is authenticated by many researchers. It is echoed by many of the women whose stories I have listened to. And their stories are even more convincing than the statistical data. Child sexual abuse is almost always related to deep and lasting pain which may affect every aspect of life: physical, emotional, relational, and spiritual.

At age thirty-five and a wife and mother, I am experiencing pain, anger, and confusion as a result of being an incest survivor and later, a rape victim. I feel flayed to the core of my spirit.

Let us examine the various areas of a person's life which lie under the shadow of child sexual abuse. (Figure 2.1 shows one way of understanding the links between some of the long-term effects of abuse.)

Physical Problems Resulting from Child Sexual Abuse

The possible immediate physical consequences of child sexual abuse are spelled out by Dr. Marvin Blumberg. They range from feeding and sleeping disturbances in infants and toddlers to bed-wetting in young school-age children, and such gynecological disturbances as dysmenorrhea (painful menstrual periods) and amenorrhea (absence of periods) in adolescent girls. Vulvar lacerations, and abrasions in the genital region, and, occasionally, venereal and other sexually transmitted infections may result from sexual contact.

In adolescence, abuse may result in pregnancy, leading either to childbirth or abortion, both highly traumatic for a teenage girl. A poignant story of incest resulting in pregnancy and childbirth at age thirteen is told by a young Christian woman in *Carol's Story*.

But the immediate physical effects are often only a prelude to lingering physical problems.

> I wonder if the very early and rough treatment I experienced had anything to do with my periods never being normal.

The Emotional Geography of Incest[7]

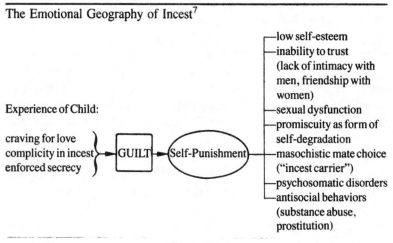

Figure 2.1

* ❋ *

I have been treated for PMS (Pre-Menstrual Syndrome) which my doctor links to the child sexual abuse I experienced.

Kathy, the nurse whose continuing story we will follow through the early chapters of this book, is under observation for possible cervical cancer after abnormal cells showed up on a routine Pap smear. "If, after all I have suffered, I should have to pay for my uncle's sin in this way, too, I don't know how I would handle it," she says. She knows that frequent early intercourse can be a predisposing factor in the incidence of cervical cancer.

Some of my sources cite obesity as a response to sexual abuse. Psychiatrist Karin C. Meiselman speculates that there may be a link between obesity and incestuous experience, although her sample was not large enough for any definitive conclusion.[8] Since being overweight may make a woman less attractive, it can serve as a means of withdrawing from sexual activity, a sort of protective covering up for the person. One woman says:

> After early sexual activity with my brother and his friends, I became very overweight. I am actually surprised to find myself married. I didn't think I would ever find anyone that could love a fat person.

The paradoxical craving for love/withdrawal from intimacy is evident in her statement.

Besides these specific physical problems, many abuse survivors experience psychosomatic disorders such as migraines, stomach and skin problems, and disabling aches and pains.

Emotional Problems Associated with Child Sexual Abuse

1. *Guilt.* Over and over again, the theme of guilt shows up in the survivors' stories.

21

I'd been sexually abused by my father as a child. I can't even remember when it began. It seems it always was, and it continued until I was in the seventh grade. The guilt and shame I have carried is tremendous . . . Sometimes I feel a double guilt—that being a Christian it shouldn't have happened to me.

Enormous guilt is, in fact, the most commonly expressed long-term effect of child sexual abuse. Why do survivors feel guilty? To those who have not experienced abuse, this seems quite puzzling. But those who have been through it tell us that their guilt may be rooted in one or more aspects of their abuse experience.

Many survivors feel guilt about an imagined defect in themselves. They ask themselves, "What's the matter with me?" One woman asks, "Why me? What is it about me that seems to elicit abusive treatment from men?" As victims of child sexual abuse learn of other children who are not abused, they often conclude they are evil, or have done something evil to attract sexual attention. This guilt is often reinforced by professionals who may ask questions which suggest that the child invited the sexual attention of the adult.

As Kathy's story illustrates, guilt also arises from the "complicity problem." Since sexual stimulation is pleasurable, survivors very often feel guilt—not only about being involved in the sexual activity but also about their pleasure in it.

As time went on I came to enjoy the sensation he made me feel despite the guilt. I even made myself available to him. I have lived with enormous guilt because I was willing to take part in this sin with my father. Do I deserve this guilt I carry?

If the child who is abused takes the place of a legitimate sexual partner (for example, her own mother), guilt may also arise from having taken another woman's mate.

I felt like a mistress throughout my teens, guilty for having sexual relations with my mother's "man."

22

Tremendous guilt is carried by survivors who wonder how they could have let the whole thing continue without telling someone. They have been locked into a sort of conspiracy against society, urged, threatened, or perhaps bribed into silence. They have, however reluctantly, shared a guilty secret (see Figure 2.2).

The guilt carried by survivors is partly an imparted guilt, laid on the abuse victim by another person's wrongdoing. It cannot be emphasized too strongly that no child has sufficient understanding to be sexually responsible. The craving for love and attention that renders a child vulnerable is the natural response of a child to trusted adults in her life. The abuse of that trust is the responsibility of the adult who initiates sexual activity. The unequal distribution of power between abuser and abused throws the weight of responsibility on the adult involved. Nonetheless, the real horror of sexual abuse lies in the fact that sexual activity is a shared experience, and the victim is stained with the guilt of it.

Why Victims Don't Tell[9]

Mary-Ellen Siemers (1986) summarizes the reasons reported by researchers for a general reluctance on the part of abuse victims to share their secret with others:

—loyalty and love for the abuser makes it nearly impossible for them to speak up against people who are supposed to be their protectors, comforters, and closest friends
—when they do get up enough courage to tell someone, the listener may respond to their revelations with horror, disbelief, judgment, or denial
—the victim is often passive because of a perception of the abuser's authority; the young child often being told that the sexual activity is acceptable but must be kept secret
—real or implied threats are often sufficient to secure passive cooperation and secrecy in the absence of any reasonable alternatives
—the severity of laws against abusers may increase the ambivalence and fearfulness of incest victims to seek help outside the family
—they tell no one simply because no one asks

Figure 2.2

2. *Shame.* Accompanying the overwhelming guilt is the feeling of shame. Women express it in words like these:

I still feel so dirty and unloved, wondering why my husband wants me.

* * *

I was molested and raped as a child of eleven years . . . All my life I have felt dirty, and worthless, and no good.

* * *

At eighteen I left home to go to a university, still feeling unclean and unworthy, a six-foot brick wall around me.

* * *

The hardest thing of all to accept is that the victim is innocent (even though she feels dirty) and deserves to be freed from the consequences of the abuse.

This sense of shame seems to be rooted in the experience of being physically overpowered and coerced into activities which are often repugnant to the child.

3. *Lack of Self-Worth and Learned Passivity.* Survivors speak of, and often demonstrate, a low sense of self-esteem, a sad and often crippling loss of self-worth as a result of child sexual abuse.

I think I must be a very dumb person because as a child I thought I had to do what everyone wanted me to do . . . And to this day I have a hard time saying "no" to people and not letting them take advantage of me.

This lack of self-worth often leads to the development of a learned "victim mentality." In *Turning Fear to Hope,* Holly Wagner Green explains the phenomenon of learned passivity:

Counselor Lenore Walker describes experiments in which laboratory animals and human volunteers were confined and then exposed to random, painful stimuli over which they had no control and from which they could not escape. Once they realized their behavior had no effect on what happened to them, their motivation to help themselves seemed to die. They ceased trying to get away or gain relief, actually ignoring obvious avenues of escape, even when these were pointed out. When they had learned they were powerless, they stopped struggling and became passive.[10]

Victims of abuse have also been exposed to random pain which could not be escaped. Many of you who are reading this book were victims in the past; that past still victimizes you. You need to have someone stand next to you, to hear someone say, "There is hope. *You can be helped.* Hundreds of others before you have sought help and found it. The power of Christ can reach into all the abnormalities and perversions that humans can devise and make things right. I believe this because I have seen it happen. It can happen to you."

4. *Anger and Hatred, Leading to Depression and Despair.* An enormous anger burns in many survivors. Quite rightly, they feel defrauded.

The intensity of my anger is brutal and potentially self-destructive.

* * *

Thank you that I can be angry . . . I think I can finally start to live. I can look people in the face. And if I want to be angry at the injustice of sexual abuse, I'll be angry. And if anyone doesn't like it, that's fine.

The tragedy of anger is that it very often turns inward on the survivor, resulting in depression, despair, and suicidal thoughts or actions. Sometimes, too, it erupts in irrational fury directed toward a husband or children. Anger and hatred always use up the energy survivors need to get on with their lives. In her autobiographical *Daddy's Girl,* Charlotte Vale Allen puts it this way: "Hating takes up so much energy, so much concentration, that there's very little left to do anything else."[11]

5. *Fearfulness and Anxiety.* Once the strong sense of basic trust has

been betrayed, many survivors experience fearfulness and anxiety. Often these fears are overwhelming. Free-floating, unfocused anxiety is something which many survivors live with. Women tell us about this general feeling of fearfulness:

My sister and I were abused as children. It has been extremely hard to overcome fears which stemmed from my past . . .

* ✳ *

At age three I was molested by a man who held me on his lap. I guess I was too young to really understand exactly what was happening, but I wonder if it didn't have some effect on me—I grew into a fearful, shy, and mistrusting child, characteristics which lasted into my adult life.

* ✳ *

With my father disliking me and my older stepbrother abusing me sexually, I felt I couldn't trust God or anyone else. My life was full of fears.

For some, the fears erupt at particular moments in relationships, shadowing some of the most joyous events and stages of life.

I was sexually assaulted by my father throughout adolescence. I hated—hated—hated it. When I married . . . I thought I had the past licked. Then, when my sons became handsome teenagers I became terrified of showing them affection for fear I would feel toward them what my dad had felt toward me . . .

* ✳ *

When I was pregnant, my husband wanted a girl—and suddenly I felt these unwarranted fears that my husband would do the same things to my daughter that my father had done to me . . .

For numbers of survivors there is a special fear of intimacy, of letting anyone close. This fearfulness is often particularly directed toward males who are all perceived as possible betrayers. Obviously, such anxiety inhibits friendships, shortchanges and fragments marriages, and sometimes results in over-protective parenting. And, of course, it impedes faith, making the spiritual pilgrimage of the abuse survivor especially difficult.

3
Behavioral and Relational Problems

Kathy's Story:

Our second son was born two years later. As the pressures increased with two small children, it became more and more difficult to cope with what I was feeling. The summer I was expecting our third child, I reached a new low. Once again I became suicidal. Every day I would think of ways to kill myself—and then I would check myself, feeling that it would be unfair to leave my husband with two babies. Then I would think that maybe I should kill all three of us and leave my husband free. Time after time I would put the two little boys in the car and drive at absolutely crazy speeds, hoping that we would all be killed.

One morning during that summer when I was pregnant with our daughter, I woke up with an overwhelming desire to die. I dressed the two boys and went out to the car again. This time, I thought, I would drive the car off a cliff. But again, as I drove toward my destination, I felt, "Oh, I can't do this!"

I remembered a friend whom I had known since my early teens. I knew she was a Christian, and suddenly I thought that perhaps she could help me. I turned around and drove to her house, only to find no one at home. It was as though my one ray of hope had been wiped out.

Crying and desperate, I stumbled back from her door to the car. I knew that somehow I had to get help. I had to let somebody know what was going on inside me. I drove the car to the plaza, went into a department store, and began to steal as much as I could shove into my purse. In my distraught condition, I reasoned that if I did something bizarre enough—like shoplifting when I had lots of money in my purse and every credit card you could ask for—I would get help. The court, I thought, would surely appoint a psychiatrist.

But what happened was both more and less than what I had expected. As I left the store, I was apprehended by a security guard and taken back into the store while the police were called. Then I was taken to the police station and put into a holding cell—I and my two little boys. I was charged, finger-printed, and finally released. When my court appearance came, I went to court alone, refusing to get a lawyer. I just wanted to be punished—and perhaps, helped.

But as it turned out, the court could not have cared less about me as a person. Not a single question was asked. I was declared guilty as charged. I paid the fine and was released, worse off than I had been before. I had only added guilt to guilt.

* ✳ *

As we have seen, the inner suffering experienced by survivors of child sexual abuse has its own geography. But the damage done by the abuse reaches beyond the inner emotional life of the survivor, like a hated hand shadowing all behavior patterns and relationships.

> I spent a lot of time running away when I got older but I never found anyone I could trust enough to tell why I kept running away, why I didn't want to go home. I didn't feel like I should live.

30

* * *

Men and women that have been sexually abused are enchained in their hearts, minds, emotions, in their destructive lifestyles . . . (I was molested and raped as a child of eleven and I've been into drugs, drinking, etc.)

For survivors, understanding why they feel and act the way they do, and why they may have difficulty in establishing and maintaining relationships, may be an important step toward healing. In this chapter, we will look first at what seem to be the reasons for such wide-ranging damage to the whole person, and then at behavioral and relational problems which survivors commonly experience.

Roots of Pain

There is no doubt that child sexual abuse is a deeply damaging experience for the victim. We have already looked at some of the long-term problems which survivors have to struggle with. It would seem that the damage may stem from some or all of the following factors:

1. *Betrayal of Trust.* Since the abuser is most often a loved and trusted person in the child's life, a deep sense of betrayed trust pervades the child's view of life. Poor basic trust is a commonly observed characteristic of survivors.

2. *Interruption of Sexual Development.* This disruption of crucial psychological and sexual development naturally affects relationships. Anna Freud explains, "The abused young child . . . is not merely exposed to an unfortunate and unsuitable sexual encounter, he is also experiencing a type of stimulation for which, developmentally, he is wholly unprepared . . . He is forced into premature phallic or genital development while his legitimate developmental needs and their accompanying mental expressions are bypassed . . ."[1]

3. *Confusion of Roles.* In many cases of intrafamilial child sexual abuse, the child is forced into a premature adult role as lover-wife-partner. Caregivers on whom the child has every right to depend exploit the child's vulnerability and relate to the child in roles which are

confusing and/or terrifying to the child.

4. *Loss of Childhood*. The abused child loses the experience and the memory of pre-sexual personhood. Thrust into a world of emotional complexity, she has no opportunity to develop resources for dealing with adult life. Many survivors have lost not only those years of innocence, but even the memory of childhood. A blocking out of painful memory resulting in memory blanks is common among abuse survivors.

In Figure 3.1, I have summarized some of the problems experienced by survivors and their possible roots in the personal history of the survivor.

Variables in Degree of Damage

Why are some survivors able to cope fairly well with life while others spend their lives under psychiatric care? Naturally, there are many variables.

1. There appears to be a significant correlation between intensity of trauma and (a) the age difference between the partners and (b) the amount of coercion involved.[2]

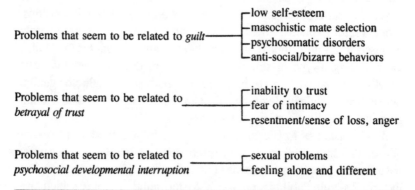

Roots of Pain
A summary of some of the long-term effects experienced by survivors of child sexual abuse.

Problems that seem to be related to *guilt*
- low self-esteem
- masochistic mate selection
- psychosomatic disorders
- anti-social/bizarre behaviors

Problems that seem to be related to *betrayal of trust*
- inability to trust
- fear of intimacy
- resentment/sense of loss, anger

Problems that seem to be related to *psychosocial developmental interruption*
- sexual problems
- feeling alone and different

Figure 3.1

2. There is evidence that sexual involvement with a family member is more disturbing than sexual experience with an unknown adult.[3]

3. There is some evidence that the younger the child when the abuse occurs, the more severe the psychological disturbance she is likely to manifest as an adult.[4]

4. The response of caregivers to a child's revelation of incest or abuse affects the long-term impact of the experience. Helen Hewitt, director of a Sexual Assault Center, tells me that there are two factors which may help minimize the damage to the child: the support of the non-offending parent offered to the child, and a confession and verbal assumption of responsibility by the offending party.

Steele and Alexander point out: "Some researchers seem to consider a person who is married and shows no serious psychotic, neurotic, or character disorder and who is living with average success within the community to have emerged from the sexual abuse unscathed. But . . . much pain and turmoil can exist beneath an outwardly normal or seemingly well-adjusted appearance."[5]

Most of the Voices we quote speak out of hidden pain.

Behavioral Problems Resulting from Child Sexual Abuse

Many victims of child sexual abuse respond by negative and self-destructive behavior patterns. They may seek escape through substance abuse (alcohol or drug addiction). Many finally run away from home, an escape route that often ends in prostitution. Judianne Densen-Gerber's rehabilitative work in seven states with young female drug abusers brought to the attention of the public the little-known fact (until then) that child sexual abuse was the first sexual experience of as many as 44 percent of the young women who sought help at Odyssey House. Many of these were involved in prostitution as well as drug abuse. It is Densen-Gerber's contention that incest is often a causative factor in anti-social behavior.[6]

Early sexual experiences often produce sexually precocious adolescents. Promiscuity is characteristic. It may be a form of self-punishment inflicted in an attempt to deal with the guilt experienced by victims. It may be a demonstration of low self-esteem or a form of further self-degradation. Or it may be a "repetition compulsion" in which,

33

paradoxically, the teenager seeks to relieve the experiences by repeating them. This seems to be the opposite of what is expected as a response to negative experience, but these researchers suggest that by repetition, the young person attempts to achieve a measure of control over the experience, to work through attendant anxiety, and/or to find some replacement for the lost parent.[7]

Whatever the dynamics of promiscuity may be, teenage promiscuity is usually a cry for love and affection. Since the sexually abused girl confuses love, guilt, and sex, too often she ends up being used as a sexual object.[8] Teenagers who have received confusing signals from trusted adults about the way in which acceptance and love is expressed lack the ability to distinguish between genuine caring and casual sex.

Of course, various forms of "acting out," often including drug abuse, may be the child's way of finally getting even with parents who have failed to give her the kind of care she needed.

Obviously, behavior aberrations such as substance abuse, general rebelliousness, and promiscuity complicate the problems of low self-esteem, guilt, and a general sense of lack of control over life and destiny. By the time some adult survivors are trying to put the pieces of the puzzle of life into some kind of meaningful arrangement, the pieces are often not only jumbled but also scarred and twisted.

Relationship Problems
The distorted relationships of a childhood marred by abuse also cast their long shadow across adult relationships in many areas.

> The memories have inhibited my marriage and ability to get really close and have a lot of trust in my husband . . .

* ✳ *

> Little did I know that sexual abuse was the root of my sexual and most of my marital problems . . .

* ✳ *

> I'm afraid to let anyone get really close to me.

34

1. *Marriage*. The betrayal of trust during childhood often makes it difficult for survivors to trust a man sufficiently to enter into a really intimate marriage. Ambivalent feelings about sex, running the whole range from aversion to addiction, often lead to problems in sexual adjustment within marriage. What is clinically called "sexual dysfunction" may be experienced as lack of response or "sexual deadness;" the experience of orgasm but without enjoyment; the ability to experience arousal contingent on being able to control the situation; flashbacks accompanied by feelings of humiliation, guilt, anger, resentment, and bitterness.[9]

Sexual problems may include vaginismus, a condition in which muscles near the vaginal opening contract involuntarily, making penetration painfully difficult or impossible. Flashback memories may be triggered during intercourse. (As one woman put it, "Suddenly, it wouldn't be my husband, but my father.") Such waves of repugnant memories often cloud the marital sexual relationship with conflict and pain.

Since fully realized sexual communion is an extension of intimacy, the poor basic trust of many abuse survivors interferes with the development of mutually enjoyable marriage.

I seldom enjoy sex. I always wonder, "Does he love me or need me?"

* ✳ *

I cannot fully enjoy sexual intimacy with my husband—in fact, I'm really turned off. I do have intercourse with him, but it's more out of duty . . .

* ✳ *

My husband tells me he doesn't blame me, but somehow I'm never sure that I can believe him.

* ✳ *

I have a hard time believing anyone could really love me. I think my husband is tired of trying to convince me that he does.

The anger the abused person has felt—and may continue to feel—toward the abuser may be generalized into a hostility against all men. Repressed anger may express itself in sudden outbursts of irrational anger.

> I've had angry outbursts all through our marriage and felt used by my husband, without knowing why. Only recently, through therapy, I have begun to remember previously blocked memories of being fondled by my father.

Many women are fearful of revealing their past to their husbands, some keeping their painful secret for many years before marital difficulties force them to seek counsel and frequently to share their whole story with their husbands.

> I was afraid to tell my husband about my incestuous past for fear he would reject me. After therapy, when I finally told him, I kept waiting for him to say, "Why didn't you stop it?" but he never did. He never thought it was my fault.

✳ ✳ ✳

> I finally sought counseling with a Christian psychotherapist for marital difficulties. I was finally able to talk about the past and even in sessions with my husband to relate to him my experience. My husband was wonderful, and together we worked out this problem . . .

✳ ✳ ✳

> We had been married a dozen years before I had the courage to tell my husband. He never said a word; he just took me in his arms and very tenderly made love to me.

Clearly, many survivors are married to caring—if often puzzled—husbands. But others face another range of marriage problems. Many abuse survivors marry abusive, domineering, untrustworthy men, thus perpetuating the abuse cycle in their own lives and often in the lives of their daughters. Low self-esteem is a factor in making poor partnership choices:

I thought that all I could deserve was a nerd—so I married one.

* ❋ *

I couldn't believe that, with my past, I could deserve to have a Christian husband and a happy home . . .

The "repetition compulsion" described earlier may also dictate the choice of an abusive husband. Whatever causes it, this pattern of choosing unworthy men to love has been noted as a frequently recurring pattern in the lives of many incest and abuse survivors. Meiselman notes, "the women . . . were not usually perceived as actively inviting abuse, but their willingness to tolerate mistreatment allowed them to endure relationships that a more mature, assertive woman would have ended or never begun at all."[10] In *The Broken Taboo,* Justice and Justice write:

Sometimes . . . daughters from incestuous families will pick husbands who are indeed untrustworthy, immature, and unreliable. It is as if these are the only kind of men to whom they know how to relate. In a sense, the daughters . . . create a self-fulfilling prophecy. They expect to find men untrustworthy and they marry men who are just that.[11]

The women who have shared their stories with us are quite frank about this repeating cycle of abuse:

My first husband was a homosexual, and my second was physically violent with me for many years before I left him.

* ❋ *

I was sexually and physically abused in my adolescent years . . . Then I was physically, emotionally, and mentally abused by my husband. I'm now divorced, trying to live a peaceful life.

* ✳ *

It seems as though I wear a sign around my neck that says, "Go ahead. Victimize me."

Women who have been victimized as children and have learned passivity as a response are typically what researchers call *incest carriers*. That is, they marry the kind of men who abuse wives and children, and in their inability to defend themselves and/or their children, create a setting for such abuse that becomes a repeating cycle.

While problems in marriage relationships may loom larger than other relationship problems, it is a fact that sexually abused children often experience difficulty in any and all relationships. Many are mistrustful of people in general—and men in particular. Anger and hostility originally felt toward the abuser is generalized in a "chip on the shoulder" attitude toward everyone they know.

A lack of self-worth may mean that the abuse survivor has an excessive need of affirmation from others. And while she may crave affirmation, she may also discount any offered words of encouragement or praise. ("Oh, really? He's just saying that.") Words flung at a child during the growing up years—"you're a no-good, just like your daddy," or, "if people knew what you were like, they wouldn't have anything to do with you," continue to haunt the adult survivor. Badgered by self-doubt, she may be unable to believe that people really like her.

I believe that a number of people truly respect me. And I know that my husband and children dearly love me. But I have trouble believing that anyone really likes me.

2. *Lesbianism.* For some abused women, the strong mistrust of men may lead toward lesbianism. A relationship with another woman may feel like a safer kind of sexual attachment. This link between child sexual abuse and homosexual practice has not been adequately understood or researched, but many women told me of homosexual experiences in their search for love. Meiselman found that seven of the twenty-three daughters in her sample who had experienced incest had

"become gay or had significant experiences or conflicts centered on homosexual feelings."[12]

3. *Parenting.* In parenting, the abuse survivor may have to fight two opposing tendencies: repeating abusive patterns of behavior, and reacting by over-protectiveness. We learn parenting from our parents. The abuse survivor works from poor models and is often unsure of herself. In addition, she may be mistrustful of all adults who relate to her children, or even openly suspicious of her husband as he relates to their daughters.

And, of course, survivors have difficult relationships with the parents who failed to give them the kind of care they needed as children. Many are torn by conflicting emotions toward their parents—feeling both love and hatred, both forgiveness and anger.

"Flayed to the core of my spirit," is how one of our Voices has already described herself. Many survivors will identify with her. For most people, relationships are at the very center of life. Child sexual abuse casts a long, dark shadow across relationships far into adult life. Many survivors respond to their difficulties in destructive ways. Depression may deepen to suicidal intensity. Living out what often seems to be a ruined life, many survivors struggle to find the strength to meet life on a day-to-day basis.

Certainly these women have earned the right to be heard. I stand in awe of their ability to survive, their tenacity in building and rebuilding their lives and relationships. The church must listen, and respond as a family to abuse survivors.

The Church Can Help

For survivors, the greatest need is to be accepted, loved, and affirmed as persons of worth. The church is uniquely endowed by the Spirit of God to become this place of acceptance. To be received and loved as a person is the beginning of wholeness. And once the church begins to recognize its responsibility and grace-granted ability to offer affection apart from sex, to meet the need of abuse survivors "to be affirmed as individuals independent of their sexuality,"[13] it will also, we hope, find its voice. For the church must not only listen to, but also speak for, these courageous survivors.

4

The
Shadowed
Spirit

Kathy's Story:

During my teen years, I did go to church quite regularly. I had found
an evangelical church near our new home and began attending. I heard
the gospel explained clearly as I became a part of the Sunday school
and youth program. I gave full intellectual assent to the truth that God,
in his great love for me, had sent his Son, Jesus Christ, to die for my
sins. I believed, too, that Jesus rose again from the dead, and that he
could offer eternal life to those who would come to him.

I responded with an invitation to Jesus to come into my life, making
a sort of initial commitment of my life to him. But that did not really
affect my life. I was a very confused person. I was, for instance,
sharply aware that my dating behavior did not tally with a Christian
commitment. My past was completely undealt with.

When I did finally get some psychiatric help after my suicide attempt,
the psychiatrist blamed the church for making me feel guilty. Instead

of helping me face my guilt, he suggested that since the church made me feel guilty, I should stop attending. (I have to make some allowance for the doctor; I had withheld the most important facts from him, so his assessment and treatment were limited and ineffective.)

I took his advice and stopped going to church. Yet although I drifted far from my spiritual moorings, I somehow knew that the answer lay, finally, with God. Meanwhile, my confused and miserable life went on.

*** ✳ ***

Like Kathy, many survivors of sexual abuse have intense spiritual conflicts which may be little understood by those who have not experienced their pain.

> Help! Sometimes I think my life is over and have thoughts of suicide. I'm a believer but feel that even God hates me and without him there's no meaning to life . . .

It is not surprising that something as traumatic and disruptive as child sexual abuse should have implications for spiritual life and growth. We are not merely "spirits within a body," but persons integrated in such a way that what affects the body also affects the spirit.

The spiritual dimension of recovery from child sexual abuse has not been explored by research. The Voices in our sample spoke out clearly from *within* the church. These people identified a number of specific areas of spiritual struggle which they relate to their experiences of molestation.

> I don't feel God really loves me—and I've been willing to accept that because I haven't felt that I deserved his love . . .

*** ✳ ***

> When I was young, I was abused by my stepfather. It has short-circuited all my attempts at a relationship with God . . .

Sadly, the church has, as a whole, shown very little comprehension of the problems faced by sexual abuse survivors. A quick prayer, a pat

Scripture text, and we expect that deeply wounded people will somehow be healed.

My Christian friend tells me I should be more up than down if I truly love Jesus as my Savior. She comes across as very condemning of me.

Charles Colson speaks of this attitude in his essay, "On Christianity and Magic Wands":

. . . much of today's teaching and preaching communicates Christianity as an instant fix to all of our pains and struggles. Consequently, we begin to think of our faith as a sparkling magic wand: we wave it, and presto, our problems are gone in a puff of smoke . . . this is, bluntly put, heresy . . . It not only makes Christians incredibly naive in approaching complex problems, but it can shatter the fragile faith of the believer who expects the magic wand to work every time. When those problems don't disappear . . .he questions whether his spirituality is faulty. The result is guilt . . . If we trust this fairy-tale brand of Christianity, we eventually fall victim to its consequent paralysis . . . as we confront our own repeated sins and failures, [and] also as we encounter the stumblings of those to whom we minister.[1]

The simplistic idea communicated in the church that "Jesus is the answer" may often be begging the question. Of course we believe and affirm this to be the case—but not in any easy, superficial way, built on repressing memories and pasting on false smiles. We believe in the deep work of his healing, resurrection life.

Learning to Trust

Survivors of abusive childhoods have some especially difficult problems with coming to faith as well as with living a faith-filled life. We have already commented on the deficiency of basic trust which characterizes many survivors. Obviously, this impaired ability to trust anyone interferes with a person's ability to become a Christian. When trust is affirmed again and again during the growing-up years, a person may occasionally recognize and have to deal with fears that crop up like occasional weeds in a field of flowers. But for a person who has had her trust betrayed consistently, a general attitude of fearfulness develops, with only an occasional bloom of faith in the weed-filled garden of the spirit. In our lives, however, we grow what we cultivate, and even a tiny, mustard seed-sized bit of faith can grow into a life-changing belief in God and his goodness. For the abuse survivor, the process of making an emotional commitment to God and nurturing that faith may be a long and demanding concern.

> I must have "received" Jesus literally hundreds of times, but I never had any assurance that he had really come into my life.

Then, too, a relationship with God demands an open transparency, an honesty about one's own personhood, which may be difficult for abuse survivors. They are mask-wearers, hiding behind carefully constructed facades. They are skilled at keeping relationships safely at an arm's length. Becoming vulnerable to anyone, God included, may cause great anxiety and deep misgivings.

When fathers and father-figures have caused the abuse, the problems with coming to Christian faith are even greater.

> I was never able to see God as "Abba" or to have a real understanding of God as Father . . . I never let anyone into my place of safety because I felt I wasn't worth it—and besides, I couldn't even trust God not to hurt me.

How tragic that fathers—some of them Christian—would do the very thing that would deface the divine image for a child.

How can one learn to trust a Father God when an earthly father has been an exploiter? It may not be easy, but as the character of God emerges from Scripture study, new understandings begin to take hold. The steadfastness of God's love is the theme of the writers of the Psalms; again and again they celebrate it. He is the Holy Father to the fatherless, and the One who can heal the crippled faculty of faith in the torn hearts of abuse survivors.

The loving embodiment of faithfulness in God's children can help the survivors come to an understanding of the goodness of God. The loyalty of Christians as surrogate family can help to remodel family roles. The love of brothers and sisters in Christ can rebuild shattered self-esteem. And a deepening understanding of the Scriptures can help the survivor build a new life.

Overcoming Guilt and Guilt-Feelings

The intense struggle with guilt and guilt-feelings which most abuse survivors experience has, of course, deep implications for their spiritual lives.

> I still have trouble believing God can't see the things I've done wrong and trouble understanding that Christ's death erased the sins. They say it will come in time . . .

* ✳ *

> I was molested by a babysitter when I was three or four; when I was nine I was raped by my brother and sold to his friends. Hate for my brother grew along with my lack of self-respect. I went to Bible College still feeling unclean and unworthy of a Christian man and home . . .

We have already discussed some of the reasons for the overwhelming guilt experienced by most sexual abuse survivors. "Amid her craving for love, her seemingly voluntary involvement in the incest, her possible enjoyment of it, and her complicity in the cover-up, the victim comes away . . . with overwhelming feelings of responsibility and guilt."[2] And in chapter six, we will talk in some detail about entering into a sense—as well as a state—of being fully forgiven.

For the abuse survivor who desires to enter into a full Christian experience, the issue is a crucial one. Francis Schaeffer's words about guilt are particularly applicable to survivors with guilt confusion:

There is a danger that the orthodox Christian will fail to realize that at times guilt-feelings are present when no true guilt exists. Let us remember that the Fall resulted in division not only between God and man, and man and man, but between man and himself. Hence there are psychological guilt-feelings without true guilt. In such cases we must show genuine compassion.[3]

Of course, for the adult survivor, as with any human being, there will be sin that needs to be confessed and turned away from. We have all sinned. We all need forgiveness, cleansing, the chance to start anew.

The rough and careless hand of another may have spilled the ink that stains my carpet. But it is still my carpet. And it is still stained and in need of cleansing, like those who have been stained by sexual abuse. Fortunately, the words of Scripture come with reassurance: ". . . the blood of Jesus . . . purifies us from all unrighteousness" (1 John 1:7,9). The sacrifice Jesus made on the cross is sufficient to cleanse from all that defiles me: my own sin, the sin of another against me.

The ancient rite of absolution is the means by which the Church traditionally has spoken the words of forgiveness guaranteed by the death of Christ. Today the words of absolution may need to be spoken by a doctor, a counselor, a friend. Dr. John White, psychiatrist and author, tells of such a case. A severely depressed man had failed to respond to normal psychiatric treatment. White found that he was troubled by things he remembered as sins.

"What about forgiveness?" I asked him.
"I want it so bad."
"What's your religion?"
"Russian Orthodox."
"And what does your priest say about how you get to be forgiven?"
"He doesn't talk too much. We go to confession."
"And what does that do?"
"I don't often go."
I groped for words. "But if you do go, why would God forgive you?"
"Because Christ died. He shed blood."

"So?"

"I'm too bad for that."

Unaccountably I grew angry. No logical reason. It just happened. "What d'you mean you're too bad?"

His voice was rising like my own. "I don't deserve ever to be forgiven."

"You're darn right you don't! . . . Who d'you think you are to say Christ's death was not enough for you? Who are you to feel you must add your miserable pittance to the great gift God offers you? Is his sacrifice not good enough? . . ."

Dr. White reports that, at this point, realization dawned on the man and he began to cry and pray at once: "God . . . I didn't mean to offend you . . . God, thank you . . . It's amazing . . . I didn't know it worked like that . . . Thank you. Thanks an awful lot. Gee, God, thank you."[4]

And from that moment, the man moved toward health and wholeness.

The person whose conscience has been stained needs to enter into understanding about:

1. The responsibility of the adult initiator for the sexual abuse. (Meiselman says, "Nothing that a child does justifies sexual approaches from a parent . . ."[5])

2. The reality of one's own sinfulness.

3. The incredible power of Christ's sacrifice to atone for sin and "cleanse our consciences from acts that lead to death, so that we may serve the living God!" (Hebrews 9:14, NIV).

For some there may be a strong emotional accompaniment to forgiveness: a feeling of release, or, as Kathy describes it, "a cool, clean breeze blowing through me." For others, there may be no particular feeling. God's forgiveness is a fact to be received by faith. It is an objective truth that "if we confess our sins, he is faithful and just and will forgive us our sins" (1 John 1:9, NIV). God's forgiveness is rooted in *who he is* and in the *provision made for us* in the death of Jesus on our behalf. It does not depend on how we feel.

This is particularly important to grasp when the whole emotional self has been wounded by abuse. The abuse survivor has to look beyond herself to find reference points. We suggest again that Scripture provides such reference points—stars to steer by even when any sense of direction is otherwise lost.

Difficulty in Receiving Love Messages

The low self-esteem which characterizes many survivors of abuse often interferes with receiving love messages from other people as well as from God.

> I was molested at nine years of age and still, more than fifty years later, I live under the burden of this awful abuse, feeling dirty and unfit before God.

✳ ✳ ✳

> I figured at one time that God couldn't love me and that I was going to go to hell no matter what I did so it didn't matter if I lived or died.

In an earlier chapter we talked about the survivor's need for excessive reassurance. It is this same need for more-than-reasonable reasssurance

---

Something You Can Do Right Now

Here are some Scripture passages for you to read, meditate on, think through, concerning the truth of God's forgiveness. As you make them your own through reading and re-reading, and perhaps through memorizing, you will come to know the truth of God's forgiveness even if you have no particular accompanying feeling just now. Joy will spring from the truth as you accept it and make it your own.

Scriptures about Forgiveness

1. Provision is made for our forgiveness in the atoning death of our Lord: 2 Corinthians 5:21; Isaiah 53; 1 Peter 2:24
2. Forgiveness is rooted in the faithfulness and justice of God: Romans 3:23-26; 1 John 1:8-10
3. A prayer for forgiveness: Psalm 51
4. A celebration of forgiveness: Psalm 32; Revelation 1:5-6

and reinforcement which interferes with confidence in one's spiritual life. Fortunately, the promises and assurances of God are written—and can be read as many times as needed until the truth washes through the mind and reaches the shadowed spirit. I have often suggested that key Scriptures be written out on note cards and placed on mirrors, refrigerator doors, cupboards—wherever they are accessible for frequent re-reading, memorizing, and meditation.

Lack of Understanding and Compassion Within the Church
As we have noted, survivors of abuse have often found little acceptance and support within the Christian community.

. . . the abused most often turn away from God; and when we have sought God, often we are further abused emotionally by the children of God. The Church does not understand our pain.

✳ ✴ ✳

It has been a struggle finding answers to the effects of the abuse I suffered in my home. The church seemed only concerned with its "name" and did not try to help me when I needed and approached it . . .

You may want to write out your transactions of forgiveness, either in this book, or on a piece of paper, or in a journal. Be very specific. Write:

Lord, I have sinned. This is the name of my sin: _____ .
I am truly sorry. Please forgive me and make me clean. Help me to hear in my heart those words you spoke so often, "My child, _____ ,
your sins are forgiven you." Amen.

Lord, this person has sinned against me. I forgive _____
for _____ . I am willing to take the pain. In my mind's eye, I am going to stand at the foot of the cross and hear you say, "Forgive him, for he knows not what he did." I am going to bring my pain and place it before you. I bring it to you; now take it from me, and release me from its weight. Amen.

49

* ✳ *

People in churches today don't want to know about "abuse." They seem to feel it is the victim's fault. How sad.

* ✳ *

I did have one counseling session with my pastor but it seems he thinks this should have healed me.

It is ironic that the Church, which should represent the compassion and the power of Jesus Christ in the lives of wounded, brokenhearted people, has so sadly failed to listen and respond. There is little doubt in my mind that the long-time male domination of the Church has left it crippled in ministering to women who have been hurt by men. But we are beginning to listen, beginning to hear. The Voices are coming through. And by encouraging, comforting, and journeying with the abused as friends, we can help each other press on.

Something You Can Do Right Now

1. Look up Romans 5:1-12. Put your name in appropriate places in these verses. The truth that comes through the Scriptures is that God's love is extended to us as we are. And so there is hope.
2. Practice accepting loving, encouraging words from others, instead of deflecting them. You will find that gradually the darkened rooms of your spirit will open to the warm sunlight of love as expressed in God's Word and world, and as modeled in at least some of the people in your life.

5

Claiming
the
Past

Kathy's Story:

After our daughter was born, we moved to another area, and I thought, "Oh, good. A fresh start. I won't have to drive by that store where I shoplifted. I'll never have to see that courthouse again." It was like I was going into a new world, and things would be different. You kid yourself into thinking a new environment will make the old one go away.

But I soon found that my problems had moved with me. I had a fourth child, and when he was about three months old I found myself again in terrible depression. The old suicidal feelings were overwhelming. One day, in desperation, I phoned a minister from a local church. I didn't know him and he didn't know me. But he came, and for the first time I told my story. The whole story.

I'm sure it was good for me to finally say it. But once I had told him, he didn't seem to know what to do for me. He just said a quick prayer and left.

As he went out my front door, I ran up the stairs, crying. I got down by my bed on my knees, crying out, "God, I don't know if you are real. I don't know if you are there. But if you are real, you are going to have to do something because I don't know what to do. I don't know where to turn."

After I had prayed and cried and become silent, I became very clearly conscious of a single phrase: "Be still and know that I am God."

I didn't even know that this was a line of Scripture. I just grasped those words like a lifeline. I lived on those words for a whole year. When flashbacks flooded over me, I said them: "Be still and know that I am God." I quoted them when anger rose like an animal inside me, raging for release. "Be still. Be still and know that I am God." After doing this many times a day for several days, I began to realize that something was changing. The spaces between flashbacks were getting longer, and one day I realized with joy, "It's been two or three days . . ."

And then a friend invited me to a women's Bible study. At first, I didn't go regularly, just once in a while. They provided babysitting, and if for no other reason, it was worth my while to have someone look after my four kids for a morning. A few months later, my friend invited me to go with her to a Christian conference. I really didn't want to go. I didn't think I could stand a whole day of religion. But I ended up going . . .

* ❋ *

As we continue to follow Kathy's story, we note that she has now taken a very significant step. She has told somebody about her past, and by verbalizing it she has claimed it as her own.

Every one of us is a sum total of past experiences and perceptions. When we cut ourselves off from our pasts, we cut ourselves off from our own identities. We are less than whole. The whole and healthy person embraces both past and future.

But for abuse survivors with their pain-filled and blighted childhood memories, a lot of courage is needed, and often the help of a counselor or therapist, for them to be able to say, "This is what happened to me. This is also a part of my life. This, too, I will claim as part of my story." Many abuse survivors have repressed distressing memories so completely and for so long that there are large memory gaps in their personal histories.

I am a recovering alcoholic. I was sexually molested by my father and oldest brother from the time I was eight until I was fourteen. The molestation only came out in therapy. I had subconsciously blocked it out—and it is causing a lot of pain and depression for me.

* ✳ *

I was sexually and physically abused as a child and God is helping me remember more about the abuse, thus creating healing after thirty years of blocking out that anything happened to me.

* ✳ *

I kept the secret of my childhood molestation within me until I was in late mid-life. I suffered torment all those years—had a nervous breakdown in my thirties and even attempted suicide in my early fifties. I have now told my family and feel released after many years of suffering . . .

* ✳ *

My first sexual experience was at age four. I just spent the last year and a half in therapy. It was a real struggle to face the truth. A part of me didn't want to accept it.

* ✳ *

I, too, am a victim of sexual abuse. It has only been in the last three years that I was able to talk about it, as I had kept it hidden inside me for over twenty years. Even though I thought I had "gotten over it," and no one else knew about it, the scars were there and it finally had to come out.

If you are an abuse survivor, an important first step toward your healing is to put words to your past, to verbalize it to another person. A young woman who leads an Incest Survivors Group told me, "It's very important to be able to tell what happened to you, to talk about it in any kind of language you want to use. It's a way of saying, 'Yes, it did happen. But it's not my *whole* story.' "

Paying Attention to Painful Memories

The subconscious mind can be compared to a large house with many rooms. When pain from the past is locked away and not dealt with, some closets or rooms are sealed and no longer available to us as spaces for living, for loving. Reclaiming our pasts means opening up all those closed places in our lives. Fortunately, God has given us a "tidy housekeeper," a natural cleansing agent within our subconscious which tries to draw our attention to the boarded up places of our lives.

Here are some of the ways in which our attention may be drawn to problems by our subconscious:

1. *Dreams*. Recurring dreams, especially those that have repetitive symbolic patterns accompanied by emotionally-weighted significance, may be an eruption into the conscious mind of concerns buried deeply in the subconscious. In *Daddy's Girl*, Charlotte Vale Allen tells of a nightmare that continued to haunt her long into adult life, a nightmare in which she is threatened by a man with a knife.[1]

The phallic symbolism, the emotional terrorism, of that dream is pretty obvious. Through dreams, the subconscious mind may be issuing an order: "Pay attention. There is something I am trying to remind you of, something locked away that is not yet resolved."

2. *Erratic behavior*. Inexplicable rage, such as the anger Kathy describes as "an animal inside me, raging for release," is something that many abuse survivors experience. When anger seems to explode out of proportion to the incident that triggered it, one needs to ask whether its true source is hidden away in the inaccessible regions of the memory. Sudden feelings of self-hatred or unreasonable intolerance are other clues to buried problems. (One woman told me of having an overwhelming aversion to a son-in-law who reminded her of her childhood abuser. Once she realized why she felt that way toward the inoffensive young man her daughter had married, she was able to deal with her feelings about him.)

Kathy's wild driving and shoplifting are examples of bizarre behavior triggered by subconscious factors—but remarkably typical in stories told by abuse survivors.

3. *Physical illness or psychosomatic pain*. When the mind is troubled by painful memories, the body may well suffer—as Shakespeare showed us so memorably in the illness of Lady MacBeth.

When we experience illness for which there is no apparent physical explanation, we should listen for the signals that are coming to us of wounds that need to be healed, of memories that may be haunting us because they have never been allowed to surface and be dealt with.

If we understand how the subconscious works to try to help us deal with long-buried problems, we should feel no embarrassment at discovering a psychosomatic illness. Instead of feeling apologetic, we should heed the signal, even respond with, "If this is a clue, if this pain (this headache, stomach cramp, burning, dizziness) is an indicator of some deep turmoil within me, how fortunate I am! What kind of intriguing possibilities of self-knowledge lie ahead?

But Do I Have to Talk About It?

It all happened so long ago. I don't even want to think about it, let alone talk about it. Why do I have to talk about it now?

There are a number of reasons why speaking of the past is helpful and may well be a first step toward healing. As we discussed in the first part of this chapter, it helps to accept your own past as a fact—you were abused as a child. It must be acknowledged. Second, there is a catharsis, or purging, of painful memories in the telling. In a book called *Carol's Story,* author Chip Ricks records the pain-filled life story of a sexually abused girl. Carol's voice says:

. . . having suffered from the deep wounds of child abuse . . . I realize that my story must be told not only for others' sake but for my own, as part of the healing process God, the Great Physician, has for me . . . I have always sensed at moments of crisis in my life that I had to face the truth and tell it in its entirety, no matter how painful the process. I know that only the truth, bitter as it is, can make me whole and set me free.[2]

This is not to suggest that a survivor should talk to just anyone about the past. A close friend can be a listener, but it is probably most wise to chose someone who can be trusted with a secret. For some, a trained counselor or therapist will be the best choice—and we'll look at how to choose and find such a person in a later chapter.

I did find an excellent Christian counselor . . . Bringing the abuse to the front where I could face it was the difficult part. I do want to explore my past, but oh, it hurts so much!

* * *

I admire those who can talk about it. I still cry when I talk about the sexual abuse in my life . . .

* * *

The last two years of my life have been very hard because of my childhood story of abuse. I suppressed it for thirty-eight years and now I feel like I opened something terrible—it overwhelms me.

Many women wonder how to go about telling their husbands. Again, the real question you should ask is: Can he handle this information? Will it improve or work against your relationship? Since openness and honesty are necessary to the full development of mutuality in marriage, you—like most wives—will probably want to share your story with your husband. However, the best place to do this may be in a counselor's office, with a third party to help in creating a setting for you to share your story, and also to help your husband deal with his own grief and anger.

You may not feel that you know someone in whom to confide just now. But whether you do or not, it is helpful to begin a journal, since writing can serve as a way of verbalizing your past and getting it into perspective (see Something You Can Do Right Now).

Writing things down has a way of getting them out into the open, into the sunlight. Writing in a journal might help you prepare for sharing your story with another person—a sort of rehearsal.

Eighteen months ago I found Jesus as my own personal Savior. (I should say that he found me!) The first thing I learned is how to journal. I am beginning to understand some things. But whereas for some people everything happens quickly, for me it has been a slow deepening, learning, loving, and doing process.

What About the Anger?

. . . in my heart I want to fly, but I have these things that weight me down. The Lord and I work on them as I can handle the knowledge, and He helps me control the rage inside of me. He knows my expanse for rage—but really my true desire is to love people.

Most of the women who speak from the experience of abuse speak of the anger that burns deep within them, anger which often erupts uninvited and is often vented on undeserving targets: husbands, children, neighbors—often just about anyone within range can become the "whipping post."

Something You Can Do Right Now

Choose a notebook you can call your own. (I use coil-bound, three-ring student notebooks for my journals.) Put today's date at the top of that first clean page. Here are some ideas to help you get started.

1. You can write your journal as "The Book of My Life." You'll find helpful suggestions for chapter headings in Ron Klug's How to Keep a Spiritual Journal in the chapter titled, "Looking Backward."[3]
2. You may choose to write your journal in the form of personal letters. You can address your letters to:
   —yourself as a child
   —your own children
   —your mother or father
   —your abuser
   —God

(It's not likely that you'll actually mail the letters to any of the above, but it is helpful for you to have the sense that you are writing to somebody.)

There's not a doubt in the world about this: anger is a highly appropriate emotion as a consequence of child sexual abuse. *Of course* you feel angry—and so do those of us who have listened to your stories. I personally feel such deep anger at the thought of children whose trust is betrayed, whose innocence is plundered, that I have often had to stop my research and pray, "Oh God! Defender of the defenseless, father to the fatherless, arise and judge those who hurt these little ones."

So it's not the anger itself that is wrong. In *Anger: The Misunderstood Emotion,* Carol Tavris points out that anger is a powerful motivator to move us to change things that are wrong. "Rage, I believe, is essential to the first phase of social movement."[4] Such a rage is being felt right now as our society becomes aroused against the selfish exploitation of children. As Tavris points out:

> Anger, like love, is a moral emotion. I have watched people use anger . . . to erode affection and trust, whittle away their spirits in bitterness and revenge, diminish their dignity . . . And I watch with admiration those who use anger to probe for truth, who challenge the complacent injustices of life.[5]

To those who are angry because of their abuse experiences, I would like to suggest this. Embrace the anger. Do not deny it. "Press against the pain," and dare to call evil that which *is* evil. It is anger denied, repressed, misdirected, which does so much damage to ourselves and to others. Pushed down into our subconscious minds, anger is often what causes deep depression and uncontrolled outbursts.

There is nothing wrong with feeling angry at your violator. Nor is it wrong to feel angry with God. A young woman told me, "If I had tried to tell people in my church what happened to me, they would probably die of shock. Then somebody would have said, 'God can help you,' and I would have said, 'Well, He hasn't yet.' I can remember lying in my bed for hours praying, 'God, please stop this'—and blaming God for what was happening to me."

Why wouldn't a little child cry out, "Oh God, where were you when I needed you? Why did you let this happen?" The good news is that

God is great enough to bear our anger. He can absorb its full impact. It is safe to spend our anger against his bosom until, in the quiet, he lets us feel the pulse of his own broken heart.

Pastoral counselor Frank Lake writes:

> The cross of Christ is intended to draw upon himself the righteous anger of the innocent afflicted, who could not defend themselves or retaliate sufficiently to halt the injustice at the time and who tend therefore to delay and inevitably to displace the reaction, so that other relatively or totally innocent people suffer. Christ was crucified in order that now our anger can spend itself, obediently and in faith, hurting the one provided, the Lamb of God.[6]

Once you realize that anger is legitimate—and even healthy—once you turn it upward, instead of outward toward others or inward onto yourself, you will find yourself freed from its control.

Getting a Grip on Your Future

What I gained from our Incest Survivors' Group was this: a sense of hope, the feeling that change is within my power.

One of the most liberating things you can learn is that while your past may have been under the domination of someone else, the future is yours. You cannot change the past or erase it, but you can determine, with God's help, to prevent it from controlling your future.

A friend told me that she was learning to pray a prayer that embraced all of her life. It went like this:

> For all that is behind, thanks.
> For all that is ahead, yes.

For many abuse survivors, to pray such a prayer is like grasping a bouquet of roses firmly by the thorny stems. How can you be thankful for a childhood that has been marred and scarred by another's evil? The only way is to become thankful for who you are. Here's what one survivor says about it:

59

I thank God even for the painful things in my life because I have learned from them.

And Kathy, our storyteller, writes to me saying, "I can at last truly say that I am not sorry that it happened to me. God is working out his purposes through the pain, and I thank him."

I stand in awe of such women who have been transformed by the grace of God into persons of great dignity and beauty. They have had the courage to look into their personal nights, to claim their own painful pasts. And in the daring to trust God for a different kind of future, they have found not only healing but the glad hope of new beginnings.

6

The Freedom of Forgiveness

Kathy's Story:

The conference I attended was the turning point in my life. The speaker was Karen Mains, and she was teaching about forgiveness.

As she started talking about how our subconscious minds deal with guilt, I suddenly felt as though she was describing me—from the inside out. She explained that our subconscious mind suppresses guilt, pushing it down until finally it surfaces in various ways: in erratic behavior, in anger, in depression. I knew all too well everything she was describing.

At the end of the session, Karen had everybody close their eyes and then she began talking quietly to those of us who were hurt by other people. "You may be here today carrying the wounds of another person's sin against you," she said. And then she explained that there were two kinds of guilt: guilt that other people put on us by hurting us and sinning against us, and guilt caused by things we have done ourselves. And I was experiencing both kinds of guilt. Guilt upon guilt.

"If you are experiencing guilt of your own, ask God to forgive you," Karen said.

That was not hard for me. I was sitting there saying, "Yes, Lord, I have a lot of guilt. I ask you to forgive me now." And I sensed that he did forgive me.

Then Karen went on. "Now, if someone else has hurt you, I want you to ask God for strength to forgive that person."

I just sat there, stunned. I couldn't believe what she was saying. I thought, "She can't mean this. She can't be asking me to forgive my uncle." She kept talking about giving our past with all of its pain to Jesus, and asking him to help us forgive that individual who had hurt us.

I sat there in my seat, and in my mind I said, "No way. He doesn't deserve to be forgiven. There's no way I'm going to let him off the hook. I can't forgive him, and I won't forgive him."

And then I realized what I was saying. Here I was, just having asked God to forgive me, but I wasn't willing to extend forgiveness, to offer my uncle what I had just asked for myself.

And Karen kept saying, "Now forgive . . . forgive . . ."

My fists were clenched and I was actually gritting my teeth. I was desperately torn. But finally, reluctantly, needing God's forgiveness too much myself to hold onto this pain, I said, "O.K., then. Lord, I'm willing to forgive him."

It was a most reluctant obedience, but God honored it. It was as much as I was able to do at the time. I'll never forget that second as long as I live. There I sat in a room with six or seven hundred other women, and I felt like I was alone with God. From the bottom of my feet up through my whole body a great weight simply disappeared.

The feeling was almost indescribable—like a cool, clean breeze blowing through me. And I knew that something had happened in that moment of forgiveness. I knew that I was never going to be the same. I never talked with anybody about it. I just quietly left the conference. But I went out of there knowing I was changed.

There had been a tremendous snowstorm that day, and it took us hours to get home. When I got there, my husband was shoveling the driveway. I said to him, "My life's never going to be the same from this day on. I don't know what has happened, and I can't explain it yet, but I'm sure things are going to be different."

The inward change was soon obvious. Love, joy, peace—the very things I had longed for but never known for more than a few minutes at a time—became real for me. My husband said to the kids, "I don't know what's happened to Mommy—but we have a new Mommy in this house."

The flashbacks ceased immediately. The healing I am describing happened more than five years ago, and only twice in those five years have I ever again had a flashback. That abrupt change was inexplicable, because I had struggled with those memories all through the years. It was as though God erased a painful part of my memories.

At last I was able to tell my husband about my pain-filled childhood. He had no idea of it until about three months after my initial "freeing," when I told him about it. He was wonderful—he took it as information that would help him understand me better. What a relief to have him sharing my life fully! He had always been good to me; now my love and respect for him is simply limitless.

As for the guilt I had carried so long, there was a tremendous, immediate release. I thought, then, that this problem was dealt with forever. I didn't realize that there was deeper healing still to come.

* ✳ *

At the moment Kathy realized she could be free of the hatred and resentment that held her prisoner, she also realized she had a choice to make. She could pick up the key that was offered, open her prison of pain, and walk out, free. Or she could reject the idea. The key of forgiveness is, after all, a heavy one, and it is a painful struggle to turn it in rusty locks.

Kathy chose to take the heavy key and turn it in the locks of her soul, stiff and rusted as they were. And suddenly she was wonderfully free. Free to accept the forgiveness of God for her own sins; free from the death-clasp of her abuser on her life.

Forgiveness Is a Choice
One of the hardest things for me to do is to forgive my father. I pray about it, because I know forgiveness is important. The Lord has forgiven me, but it is very hard . . .

63

Forgiveness is a choice which each of us has the opportunity to make—not only once but many times throughout life. And each time we choose to forgive, we make a choice for freedom. Lewis Smedes says, "When you forgive someone who hurt you, you are dancing to the rhythm of the divine heartbeat . . . you are in tune with the music of the universe. You are riding the crest of love, the energy of the cosmos."[1]

"I *can't* forgive my father," a young woman says through clenched teeth. "He ruined my life." The strange paradox of the whole matter is that until she forgives her father, he (although now in jail) has the power to go on ruining her life. When she makes the choice to forgive him, his power over her life is destroyed.

In *Great Expectations,* Charles Dickens creates an unforgettable metaphor for the damage caused in a life by the failure to forgive. Miss Havisham, jilted as a bride many years earlier, sits in her horrible, cob-webbed bridal chambers, wearing her yellowed wedding dress. She explains to Pip:

On this day of the year, long before you were born, this heap of decay . . . was brought here. It and I have worn away together. The mice have gnawed at it, and sharper teeth than teeth of mice have gnawed at me.[2]

The destructive influence of her vindictive resentment in the lives of both Pip and Estella is a parable of the kind of damage that unforgiveness works. Men and women have testified that unforgiveness wreaks havoc again and again in the life of the person who harbors it, as well as in the lives of others.

The difficulty of forgiving—and the importance of it for reclaiming one's own life and for living in freedom from the control of the past—runs like a theme through the stories women have shared:

I am working with a counselor to deal with the intense emotion—mostly the anger, but also the guilt, shame, fear, pain, bitterness, and confusion I am feeling as a result of abuse. I have a problem with these negative emotions as a Christian. Christians shouldn't feel these emotions . . . forgive and forget and all that jazz . . .

* ✳ *

I know I have to deal with what happened to me as a child instead of letting it lay in darkness in my heart and fester. I must forgive . . .

* ✳ *

My parents are both dead and I went to their graves to get rid of my feelings, and I found the anger and hate are still there, so I wasn't ready to forgive him for what he had done to me.

For most of us, forgiving someone who has hurt us deeply is too hard to do without help. The choice we have to make is to be *willing to forgive*.

What is Forgiveness?
Forgiving is not excusing. Though understanding some of the reasons for abuse is helpful, no one is asking you to say, "It's O.K.—he couldn't help himself." It's *not* O.K., and forgiveness operates in clear acknowledgment that we have been hurt, that we have been sinned against. In fact, forgiving can only happen in the light of a moral judgment.

When we offer forgiveness, we do several things.

1. *We transfer the case to a higher court.* When we forgive, we file a Quit Claim. We say, "I will no longer demand an accounting."

A good definition of forgiveness is "to give up all claim to punish or to exact penalty for an offense."[3] As long as we are unforgiving, we hold the person who hurt us responsible to us. We demand an accounting. We may desire to get even, to injure the person in return for our injury. Many abuse survivors have told of harboring a desire to murder their abuser—and it's hard not to sympathize with that feeling. But it is destructive and life-threatening—not so much to the person who is hated with murderous intensity as to the person who hates and harbors the consuming desire for revenge.

In forgiving, we acknowledge the wrong done to us but commit that person to a higher Judge. We say in forgiving, "I am letting go of my desire to punish that person. I am turning him over to God." (It is something like stopping being a vigilante and turning the offender over to established Justice.)

65

2. *We let go our resentment.* A second aspect of forgiveness is to "give up resentment . . . stop being angry with."[4] This is a conscious act.

It is interesting that the word "forgive" actually comes from the very ancient roots meaning "to give away." And that is actually what we do when we forgive. We give away our resentment, our anger. I have a mental image of leaning over a bridge railing above a fast-flowing stream and heaving my resentment and hatred over the edge to be carried away by the swirl of the waters.

3. *We become willing to bear the pain of another's sin against us.* The will is the part of the mind for which we bear responsibility. Like Kathy, we often bring it to reluctant obedience to Scripture. We cry, "I can't forgive, but I am willing to try." At this point we begin to understand and experience what it is like to be Christ, the One who gasped out, in the midst of his torture, "Father, forgive them, for they know not what they do."

When the pain of our tormentor becomes real to us, and when we link it with our own willingness to take that pain and release the offender, we participate in a God-like act and suddenly understand that forgiveness is costly. It was costly to Christ who was willing to bear the pain, who willingly died, who willingly forgave, who instructed us to forgive seventy times seven.

Christ is willing—willing to bear the pain, the affront of every evil, hateful, disobedient, and selfish act you have committed. He asks that you be willing to do the same. At this point, forgiveness ceases to be simply doctrine and becomes a gripping experience.

4. *We wait for and expect God to work an act of release within.* Forgiveness is not complete until something supernatural occurs, until there is a work of release within us that could only be brought about by divine and holy action. Whenever I am dealing with people struggling to forgive, I ask them to be willing to take the pain. Then I ask them to go to prayer and see the cross in their mind's eye. I ask them to carry their burden of pain to the foot of the cross and to leave it there. That is the reality of redemption.

Waiting bowed at the foot of this death-gibbet, our pain begins to ease, cleansing tears flow, and our constricted hearts and souls loosen.

A quiet inner peace grows, a gentle inner light warms us. We have understood Calvary; now we begin to experience Resurrection.

All normal psychological responses? Perhaps, but one day soon or down the road of years, we will begin to experience a surprising compassion for the crippled, hollow, half-people who did us such harm. Impossible? Humanly, yes. But not to God, not to God.

The watershed issue of Christianity that makes it distinctly different from all other world religions is this very issue. Can we love our enemies? Can we bless those who persecute us? Can we pray for those who despitefully use us? In our humanness we cannot. But God begins to fill us with his redemptive love. He frees us through forgiveness of the effect of evil practiced against us. He begins to fill us with something akin to compassion. And this we can only call a miracle.

I forgave my father and wrote him a note for the first time in years. Before receiving my letter, he called me to ask forgiveness. I could say I already had.

* * *

I forgave my mother and father yesterday. I still don't ever want to see them again; but at least I can live with the memory of what they did. And suddenly, I feel wonderful. What a relief!

* * *

I know now why my husband wept and wept before he died. My daughters told me he had sexually abused them. At first I cursed him in my heart, but then I repented. I think I have forgiven him. That man went to the grave with these terrible acts on his soul.

* * *

I forgave my abuser and whereas before there was scarcely a day I didn't remember, now there is scarcely a day that I do.

* * *

I forgave and felt such holy inner release. It was then I understood that God was angry at them, too, but he still loved them.

67

Forgiveness is a choice. It can be dramatic; it can be slow and barely recognizable. Either way, we notice that the pain from the memory of the acts against us is diminishing. It is often an on-going process. There are many people I have had to forgive again and again. As one abuse survivor told me, "I find I have to forgive each time I remember."

Often the subconscious mind stores the living realization of past horrible acts so tightly that it needs to hear the words of forgiveness spoken with authority in order to be convinced. At this point, it may be extremely important that a trusted person hear our words of repentance, our request for forgiveness. We humans often need to hear Christ's words of absolution, "Child, your sins are forgiven you," spoken by a loving spiritual mentor. We often need a witness to hear our prayers of forgiveness so that we can mark the time and the place and say, "I know I have forgiven. I can remember the actual moment."

We may have to approach forgiveness feebly. Like Corrie ten Boom, who met one of her prison guards after World War II, we may have to pray, "Jesus, I cannot forgive him. Give me your forgiveness."[5] But the important thing is that when we are faced with the need to forgive, we will learn to forgive.

Lack of forgiveness is like a desk stacked with overdue unpaid bills. Through prayer therapy, we work our way down through the stack. And with obedient practice, there comes a time when we learn to pay the bill immediately when it comes due. We forgive as a spiritual discipline—when we are reminded of past pain, when the horrid words that wound are spoken, when someone tries to manipulate, to coerce, to use us. We forgive and are freed from the effect; and this freedom allows us to go about the process of rebuilding again the habitation of our interior, most sacred, human selves.

What Forgiveness Does For Us

Forgiveness is the only way in which we can both simultaneously embrace and be free of our pasts. Until there is forgiveness, we are locked in a painful relationship with the person who has wronged us. Our living hatred and resentment of the person keeps him present even though it may be years since we have seen him. He may be completely removed from us and still continue to ruin our lives if we are bound to him by the cords of hatred. We are, after all, slaves to the persons we hate. When we forgive, we are released from this destructive bonding.

Forgiveness also opens us fully to the forgiveness God extends to us. "Forgive us our trespasses," we recite in the Lord's prayer, *"as we forgive* those who trespass against us." Why this contingency?

If we think of the illustration of the household of the mind with rooms double-bolted, and windows boarded, then we will have a good visual picture of the effect of sin on a human soul. Into those closed rooms we have shoved the guilt of our own sins, our bitterness, our hate, our vengeful spirits as well as the memory of the pain of grievous acts against us. Until we take the key of forgiveness and tentatively push it into one of those locks and (however reluctantly) open those doors, God's love is often unable to reach our most inward, wounded selves. His light cannot shine through the dusty, shuttered windows with the shades pulled and the curtains drawn tight. All his Holy Spirit needs is one little crack, a closed thing pushed ever so slightly open, a faint cry—*I forgive.*

But he will not force himself. And for the abuse victim who has so often been encroached upon by force, that is an overwhelmingly precious reality. The Holy Spirit waits for an invitation to come into our most sacred inward selves. And at first, for many, "I forgive" is the closest to a welcome that can be given.

Look at all that forgiveness does:

1. When we "forgive those who trespass against us," we empty our hearts of hatred and make room for God's love and forgiveness.

2. When God forgives us, he is offering grace, not just as a gift for us to have and to hold, but in order that it may flow through us and on to others. By forgiving, we become channels of God's love in a love-starved world.

3. When we forgive, we act like Christ: we experience personal Gethsemanes and Golgothas. We walk the way of the the cross and share in fellowship with our Lord Jesus Christ. It is, for us, an act of obedience and of identification.

4. When we forgive, we open the festering wounds of our lives to the healing of God. As any medical person knows, only clean wounds can heal properly. That's why the first step in healing is cleansing—however painful that may be.

7

The Journey
Toward
Healing

Kathy's Story:

My initial sense of release lasted for several months. Then God began
to work in my life to make me face things in greater detail. The
overview had been taken care of, but now he and I had to take care
of the details.

I began to be involved in intensive Bible study. Up until that point,
I had been addicted, terribly addicted, to the afternoon soaps on television. I would get all my work done so that by early afternoon I could
be in the family room, maybe with mending or ironing to do, in front
of the television. When I realized how unhelpful and unhealthy these
shows were, and what a waste of time they were, I decided to give
God the same amount of time that I had given to the soaps: three and
a half hours every afternoon. I figured if I had been able to arrange
my housework so I could watch the soaps, I could now arrange my
housework to give me the same amount of time to learn the Scriptures.

At first, studying was very difficult for me. Although I had been a good student in the past, I did not find Bible study very easy nor, at first, particularly enjoyable. I literally forced myself not to look ahead at the next question in the home-study course I was working on, lest it frighten me. I'd start in and I'd say, "Lord, just help me answer this one question." And then, when I'd get it done, I'd go on to the next one.

I literally prayed my way through each study, question by question. I started with an inductive study of Philippians, a short New Testament book. Later, as my knowledge and confidence and hunger for the Word grew, I went on to study some of the great biblical themes: God's nature, his covenants with us, and so on. Gradually, I was gaining a biblical and Christian mindset. My mind was being renewed.

There were, of course, practical implications of this new way of thinking. In my marriage. In my role as mother. In my poor self-image. For example, I was still overeating—probably a carryover from self-destructive urges. I did battle on that issue and lost about forty pounds. But it was—and still is—a battle to keep that in balance, using self-discipline but not becoming obsessed with the whole thing.

And meanwhile, I realized I had to go still deeper.

A woman whom I met through the group Bible study pledged herself to me as a "prayer partner." We met regularly to pray together. The Scriptures teach, "Confess your sins to each other and pray for each other so that you may be healed" (James 5:16, NIV). I am learning that healing still comes that way.

*　*　*

Psychotherapist Susan Forward says, "Revealing a major trauma . . . is just the beginning . . . People sometimes find so much relief in the initial revelation that they leave treatment prematurely . . . When the initial euphoria wears off, the patient is still struggling with unresolved conflicts . . . Emotional purgings need to be experienced repeatedly . . ."[1]

Psychiatrist and author M. Scott Peck puts it this way: most abuse survivors "are simply seeking relief. When they realize they are going

72

to be challenged as well as supported, many flee and others are tempted to flee."[2]

Like many child sexual abuse survivors, Kathy is still experiencing an ongoing healing—an initial dramatic release followed by a sense of still needing deeper freedom from the bondage of the past. I often tell those who have had initial spiritual encounters that these incredible moments are God's promises of what the future can be. It is not for us to look back when life becomes difficult again and whine, "But God, why? You were so close and I was so free—what happened?" Rather we have a gift to hold to our hearts, a memory of beauty to make bearable the plunge into a past that continues to strangle our present.

Kathy's determination, her psychological understanding, and the faithfulness of a friend who listened to moments dark with pain and grief are remarkable. Her intense interaction with Scripture and determined prayer are tools that can be used by other abuse survivors. It is possible that one day Kathy may even discover a desire for a sustained exchange in a professional therapeutic environment—or she may not. But her determined commitment to growth assures steady, healthy results.

Other Voices recognize that maturity can be achieved only through sometimes arduous progress.

I am healing, a baby-step at a time.

✳ ❇ ✳

After three years of serious marriage problems, we went to a Marriage Encounter weekend. My husband accepted Christ, and I am on the road to slow healing.

And very realistically, many Voices recognize that while they have had and are experiencing healing, there are still scars.

I was an abused child, and although the Lord has given me great healing and an understanding marriage partner, I know the scars of my early experience are still with me.

* * *

I was abused as a child for about fifteen years by my father and brother. The scars will be with me until I see Christ.

The lack of understanding on the part of fellow-Christians with regard to the length and depth of this healing process is often a frustration to the survivor determined to discover permanent wholeness . . .

I find only too often people think you are living in the past when you speak of it . . . People say, "You should be over that by now."

. . . but the Voices also tell of discovering in Christ a rare intimacy (perhaps they have come to experience him as one of the few males who can be totally trusted) and an understanding that others are unable to give.

The sexual abuse in my childhood was severe and often my world shifted into cycles of unreality. Strangely enough, the one reality I can remember that always held (even when I was a little child) was Christ. I don't know how this happened or why especially to me—all I know is that when things were most confusing, he was there. He is still the Center . . .

A Time for Healing
Healing can be instantaneous for some; many testify to spiritually cathartic moments that hastened them toward health, allowing them to bypass certain developmental steps. But most of the time, healing is deliberate and orderly. It helps to keep in mind the analogy of physical healing. While a scratch or a sprained ankle heals relatively quickly, the multiple injuries caused by a terrible accident can take months, if not years to mend. The impact may have shattered bones, torn internal organs. First come sessions of delicate surgery. The patient is not whole when wheeled out of the operating room. Then comes a long period of recovery: the slow knitting together of flesh, muscle,

ligament, the multiplication of new cells, the removing of the old, traumatized ones. Both the wounds inflicted by the accident and the incisions made by invasive surgery must heal.

Healing takes time. Often the expectation for quick healing from the effects of early child sexual trauma is unrealistic. It is just as simplistic as thinking: Why do I have to have this tumor removed? Why won't it just go away? Why do I have to take penicillin for double pneumonia? I hate medicine. Won't I get better if I just get plenty of rest?

Some survivors want to get well without cooperating with the natural healing processes which the Divine Healer has built into the human psyche.

Damage from early child sexual abuse, from incest, is often enormous. It is also reparable. Perhaps that needs to be repeated. *It is also reparable*. But there must be an attitude of help-seeking on the part of the wounded one. Jesus still asks us, as he asked the paralyzed man beside the pool of Bethesda, "Do you want to get well?" (John 5:6). In a very real sense, it is up to us.

I asked a sexual assault counselor how I could motivate a woman to come for help. "Women like this have had so little control of their lives that it is important that they act autonomously in seeking help. All you can do is tell them of the help available, and offer your support in getting to it. Then they must act on their own behalf. If they don't we can't help them anyhow."

God usually does not help us toward health until we take one step, one action which indicates serious decision, serious desire to be well, on our part. We must seek healing at whatever level we are at—even if we can offer no more than a faint, desperate gasp, "Oh God, help!"

We begin to walk—crawl, creep, strain—toward the light, like Kathy going past a Christian friend's house, going to a Bible study, seeking out a pastor, attending a women's conference.

At some point, the individual must commit herself to the rehabilitation process. The lack of this commitment is like the child shaking his head at the teaspoon of medicine, clamping his mouth shut, spitting out the tablet, or purposefully gagging while swallowing the capsule. Without a cooperative leaning toward health, we are like little children still waiting for someone to do it for us, to take care of us, to make it all better. God does it with us and works through others on our behalf, but we must take some initiative toward health on our own.

In *The Road Less Traveled,* M. Scott Peck assures us that deciding to seek counseling or psychotherapy is one of the hardest, yet most courageous and significant decisions an individual can make.

The Determination Factor

After physical injury, atrophied muscles must be exercised, rebuilt limbs must be painfully stretched and flexed, sometimes nervous signal systems must be repatterned in order for the body and brain to coordinate. Whenever world class sports events are shown on television, there is the inevitable story about the championship athlete who last year suffered a terrible injury, or broke a leg in a skiing accident. "We thought he would be scratched from this season's competition," some newscaster invariably comments. The cameras then focus on scenes in physical therapy rooms showing the determined skier working out for hours on weight machines under the hovering attention of a medical sports therapist, building again the traumatized bones and muscles. To the whole world's surprise (the part of the world that is interested at any rate), the athlete appears in this year's skiing circuit, better than ever.

This determined action is what we must bring to the search for emotional wholeness; we must learn to grit our teeth and say, "I will be well." We must expect that God will become the surgeon who excises the malignancy of the past which threatens to spread in our souls. He will use many means in this operation—Scripture, the inner light of the Holy Spirit, loving Christians, skilled non-Christians, groups of incest survivors, the offices of the church. Healing, no matter in what form it comes, is always a part of his plan for us.

And after this holding of hands, this task which requires the rich interplay between human love and divine intervention and help, we grit our teeth and say, "I will be well, so help me God."

Divine Therapy

God is also the Divine Therapist who oversees our rehabilitation, whose hand is available for us to squeeze when the pain becomes unbearable, who makes sure if we trust ourselves to him that we won't be plunged into therapy more demanding than we can possibly sustain. But he also insists that if we are going to compete in the circuit of life's championship experiences, we must sweat, strain, and work out under his rehabilitation program.

"Do you not know that the unrighteous will not inherit the kingdom of God? Do not be deceived; neither the immoral, nor idolators, nor adulterers, nor sexual perverts, nor thieves, nor the greedy, nor the drunkards, nor revilers, nor robbers will inherit the kingdom of God. *And such were some of you.* But you were washed, you were sanctified, you were justified in the name of the Lord Jesus Christ and in the Spirit of our God" (1 Corinthians 6:9-11, RSV).

At first glance, these verses may seem discouraging to the survivors of early child sexual abuse who are hounded by self-blame and self-hate and who immediately fixate on the negative phrases—"the unrighteous will not inherit"—and actually miss this Scripture's tremendous positive implications for survivors. In the moral confusion of a sexually perverted Corinthian society, Paul gives powerful hope: *"And such were some of you,* but you were washed (made clean), you were sanctified (set apart as holy for God's special use), you were justified (made as though you had never sinned)." No one who wants to be whole, to be restored, to remember innocence again is beyond the circle of God's healing power. *And such were some of you.*

> I was molested and raped as a child. I've been into drugs, drinking, etc. All my life I have felt dirty and worthless and no good, and was told that all my life. I'm middle-aged and I'm still feeling this. I'm going to group counseling and that has helped, but I need to know how God sees me. I'm crying out to God for help.

Help comes when the abuse survivor learns how to put herself in God's way.

The Mind Renewed
To the Roman Christians, people living out their faith in a morally depraved city, Paul writes, "Do not conform any longer to the pattern of this world, but be transformed by the renewing of your mind, that

77

you may prove what is the will of God, what is good and acceptable and perfect" (Romans 12:1, RSV).

How can our minds be renewed?

1. *Scripture*. Modern social scientists have written extensively about positive behavior modification, but the Scripture has been teaching spiritual principles of attitude and behavior modification for centuries. One step toward health that abuse survivors need to take is a renewal of their minds. God's desire for them is that they will be able to focus on what is good (not what is ugly) and acceptable (not what is socially and morally degrading) and perfect (what is whole). Kathy has given us an excellent model for beginning this process—a saturation of her mind with Scripture and a participation in intensive prayer therapy. For many, however, emulating Kathy's hours and dedication will seem a mountain too rugged to climb; some women and men are over-whelmed just with the effort of living out one more day.

Be still and know that I am God . . . Although unaware that these words were from Scripture, Kathy clung to them like a lifeline tossed to save her from drowning.

Often mind renewal begins with bite-sized portions, a Scripture phrase repeated over and over, a verse memorized to hold off the threatening dark. Footholds are chiseled into the mountain; handholds are discovered; we slip and catch at a strongly-rooted sapling. "The law of the Lord is perfect, reviving the soul." We rest on a a sheltering ledge. "The statutes of the Lord are trustworthy, making wise the simple." We pant, we stave off the anxiety attack from the fear of falling. "The precepts of the Lord are right, giving joy to the heart." We sleep awhile. We wake. We start the difficult ascent again. "The commands of the Lord are radiant, giving light to the eyes" (Psalm 19:7-8, NIV).

I now read the Bible every morning and every night and try to learn one verse a day out of my reading, for one's thoughts can go back to the ruts very easily if one doesn't have a full armor of strength to keep it out.

For many, it is only after this gentle, beginning rehabilitation with the Word in the survivor's battered and exhausted mind that she develops the capacity to do more. She joins a Bible study. She turns off the afternoon soaps and works through a Bible studyguide. She writes out verses on three-by-five cards and tapes them to the bathroom mirror, the refrigerator, the dashboard of the car. She begins to discover that Scripture is the ointment that anesthetizes the sting of wounds. It is the balm, the oil that eases pain, the antibiotic that fights raging inner soul disease. One simple phrase can ease the mind's torment. One memorized passage can obliterate the on-again, off-again fixation with suicide. "He sent his word to heal them and bring them alive out of the pit of death" (Psalm 107:20, NEB).

Renewing the mind has its full effect when, like Kathy, we can give ourselves to intensive study. In fact, there is a direct relationship between the effectiveness of the rehabilitation process and the amount of time we can give to Scripture. Psychiatrist Dr. John White writes in *Masks of Melancholy:*

> An . . . area where the pastoral counselor can offer help . . . is to teach and to encourage the sufferers in solid, inductive Bible study . . . Years ago, when I was seriously depressed, the thing that saved my own sanity was a dry-as-dust grappling with Hosea's prophecy. I spent weeks, morning by morning, making meticulous notes, checking historical allusions in the text. Slowly I began to sense the ground under my feet growing steadily firmer. I knew without any doubt that healing was constantly springing from my struggle to grasp the meaning of the prophecy.[3]

2. *Prayer.* Kathy worked through each agonizing memory of her past in the presence of a prayer partner. This kind of prayer work has enormous efficacy. The fastest psychological healings that I have seen have come when the abuse survivor found a good psychological counselor who believed in and used prayer in the therapeutic process. But again, this plunge into the pain may be overwhelming to many who

have spent their entire lives avoiding the memory of their sexually abused pasts.

The Lord Jesus Christ and I work on these things from the past as I can handle the knowledge. From the very beginning I showed myself and the Lord my expanse for rage—but my true desire is to love people, the Lord's creations, to love truth and knowledge. I hate this dark, covered-up side of myself, but the Lord knows how to reveal the darkness to me.

Like Bible study, prayer may be exercised in extended periods of time or in tiny life-spaces. Those who are coping with looming emotional instability may only be able to take prayer in small doses. Writing prayers down helps.

The Feeling Prayer

A simple form (daily, if possible) might begin with the *feeling prayer*— "God, today I feel so lonely. Does anyone understand my pain?" Then start listing hoped-for minimal achievements for the day—"I would like to get a decent meal on the table. I would like to spend fifteen minutes reading Scripture. I would like to go to the store without having a panic attack. I would like to go through the day without screaming at the children." At the end of each day, look back on it. Now is the time for *reviewing prayer*. Thank God for his help. Write down the small victories. "Today was better. I woke this morning and felt hope. I now finally know that you love me. I want someday soon to feel your love."

The Prayer Journal

Writing out prayers makes the spiritual journey concrete. It records the mind's sometimes small but nevertheless significant renewal. In fact, a counselor I know never agrees to counsel with an abuse victim unless she will agree to journal. Journaling is one of the methods by which we begin to achieve self-directed spiritual and emotional growth.

Recording your prayers can be an extension of the journaling process we have already encouraged you to begin.

Listening Prayer

The second type of prayer I recommend for abuse victims is *the prayer of listening*. In a later chapter I will describe this more fully. In its essence, listening prayer is so simple there is no excuse not to practice it. It is nothing more, really, than sitting before the Lord, becoming aware of his existence through a Bible portion, or going to a place filled with quietude, and then hushing one's noisy heart and saying, "Lord, what is it you have to say to me today? Here I am."

Most people can't hear God's subtle, inward voice because they are so busy crying out, so noisily demanding things from God that they never take time to hear him speak softly to them. They are like the child downstairs who comes home from school screaming, "Mom! Mom! Hey, Mom!" And each time he calls, the mother who is upstairs answers, "I'm up here! Here I am! Up here!" But the child can't hear his mother's answer above his own shouts.

Sometimes we hear nothing after we have quieted our noisy child-cries. But the silence begins to seep into our souls. Sometimes the quiet is interrupted by brain chatter—You forgot to take out the meat to defrost; you forgot to call so-and-so. I write these notes down to free my mind from worry and quiet myself again. Sometimes then I hear the quiet word, "My Beloved." That is well worth waiting for.

Answers to the questions "What shall I do? To whom shall I turn? Where can I find help?" are often found in silence. Our problem as people is not that we don't ask the questions, not that we don't cry out; but most often it is that we don't listen enough for a reply.

Prayer—how often our Voices link it to healing. An elderly man, abused as a child, spent a lifetime struggling with guilt.

I was led to John 14:27 ("Peace I leave with you; my peace I give you. I do not give as the world gives. Do not let your hearts be troubled and do not be afraid," NIV). After a long prayer upon my knees unto God I felt his peace from the top of my head to my toes, and my life has never been the same since. My guilt was removed then . . .

* ❋ *

A Christian couple lifted me in prayer for many months. Then through a Christian outreach ministry, I was led to a seminar on depression. Through many prayers . . . I was delivered from the bondage of abuse.

* ❋ *

Two years ago the Lord brought a dear friend into my life as a daily telephone prayer partner, spending ten to fifteen minutes most week-day mornings in prayer over the phone. Finally, I was able to confide in her about my dad, after I found out she had been raped in her childhood. A true healing process had begun as we prayed and cried together.

What an incredible bonding of love the prayer net is. Do any of us really utilize its healing potential?

Perhaps you might begin in prayer by praying daily, "All I know of myself I offer to all that I know of you. "Write it down. Make it concrete.

Mother Teresa describes prayer this way:

Something You Can Do Right Now
Choose the reassurance you most need and write the Scriptures out on a card that you can tape to a place where you will see it often.

Here are some Scriptures for you to meditate on:

1. To help you deal with anxiety: Philippians 4:6; Matthew 6:28-32
2. To help you deal with guilt: 1 John 1:9-10; 1 John 2:1-2; Isaiah 43:25
3. To help you know God's love: Romans 5:4-5; 1 John; John 15
4. To help you gain assurance of salvation: Romans 10:9-11; John 3:16
5. To help you sense your worth as a person: Psalm 139

You have listened as God speaks to you in his Word. Now answer him. Express your heart's response in words, using the space below.

The beginning of prayer is silence . . . God speaking in the silence of the heart. And then we start talking to God from the fullness of our hearts. And he listens.

The beginning of prayer is Scripture . . . we listen to God speaking. And then we begin to speak to him again from the fullness of our hearts. And he listens.

That is really prayer. Both sides listening and both sides speaking.[4]

And for the abuse survivor, prayer—both sides listening and both sides speaking—and Scripture, sent to heal and deliver from the pit of death, are the beginning of the renewing of the mind.

8

Seeing God
as He
Really Is

Kathy's Story:

I had to come to a new understanding of God.

My initial search was really to find out what I could about the character of God. I remember studying the attributes of God—how he's just, holy, righteous, omnipresent, omniscient. I studied what each of these words means and began to see what a great God he is.

I studied the sovereignty of God. I came to believe that God in his perfect sovereignty could have prevented what happened to me when I was five years old. That he chose not to has to be because he ultimately purposed that good should come about despite the evil that was done to me.

To be very honest, from where I am right now in the healing process, I can say I'm not even sorry that it happened because I have seen the grace of God in a marvelous way. And God has taught me so much.

Strange as it may sound, I don't know if I would undo the past if I could. I no longer have the self-pitying, "Why me? Why did I have to have my life messed up by someone else?" attitude. I have learned that his grace is greater than what happened to me. And that makes the big difference.

In my teenage years and early twenties I used to think, "No male is ever going to dominate me." I was not in any feminist groups, but my attitudes were certainly consonant with theirs.

So coming to terms with a masculine God was very important for me. I think it would be a great mistake if someone who had been through this were to think of God as female—an incorrect and unscriptural view—because they would never have to deal with their problem with the opposite sex.

When you have been through child sexual abuse, you have no respect for males. You don't trust them. So it's important to your healing to come to trust this masculine God; to honor him, to submit to him. The last thing a woman who's been defiled by a man wants is to be submissive to a man. Everything in you wants to fight men. To stand up against them. All of them.

But when you come to the Word of God, you have to come as an individual before God and submit to him. You have to honor him and respect him. And in the process, your perception of males is corrected. "They" are no longer the enemy. Evil is.

It's all quite circular and very important for redeveloping relationships. As you learn to love and trust God, you are healed in your ability to love and trust your own husband. You stop being hostile to men in their maleness.

* ✳ *

Rebuilding Worldviews Shattered by Abuse

I'm a believer but feel that God hates me and without him there's no meaning to life. Maybe I'm not even a Christian.

* ✳ *

I'm saved but it took me twelve years to realize that God could really love me, and many times I still struggle with that . . .

86

* ✳ *

I was the victim of abuse in my "Christian" family. Although I have worked through much of my past, the issue of Christianity and what it really means has continued to be a major problem for me.

I was talking with Edie, a young mother whose childhood had been full of the fear of displeasing her abusive, perfectionist father. "God's intentions toward you are loving," I reassured her. "He plans good for you."

"Oh, I know," she answered quickly. "Just as long as I don't botch them up."

In that momentary exchange, I glimpsed how difficult the matter of trust, of God's unconditional love, was for her. She had transferred her father's negative perfectionism to God. God would do good things for her, all right, but only contingent on her own efforts. In this bondage, she was trying to work out both the painful past and the stress-laden present.

Throughout childhood, we build our worldview by assimilating thousands of bits of information and building them into the framework by which we understand and adapt to the world around us. Theologians are paying increasing attention to the family unit as "the cradle of theology."[1]

And small wonder that Jesus told us to become as little children in order to enter the kingdom. Childlike trust is an essential ingredient in spiritual faith. Survivors of child sexual abuse need to completely rebuild their worldviews. They need to construct a mental model in which the father-figure, the authority figure, is trustworthy. In doing this they create a framework for real faith in God as he really is.

Child sexual abuse within the family is a form of blasphemy. It breaks the image of God for the child. "So God created man in his own image, in the image of God he created them; male and female he created them" (Genesis 1:27, NIV). When the family roles are scrambled, it's hard to separate maleness from femaleness. The normative imagery of understanding: "I am male; I am female. This is what

87

it is like to be male, to be female" no longer has any clear definition. As one victim said, "What's a father? A father's just a name, no more than a name."

Sexual abuse within the family breaks the image of God, shattering the understanding that God is like my loving father who protects me, wants the best for me, disciplines me wisely when I am wrong, loves me utterly and always in what I am and in what I am becoming. The incestuous sex act interrupts and wretchedly confuses the progression from accepting healthy human love to knowing the divine love of God.

What Is God Like?

The nature and characteristics of God are the main theme of Scripture from *Genesis* to *Revelation*. The God who very specifically warned his people not to make any engraved or pictured image of him chose to reveal himself in words—words which would be translated and passed through the centuries so that each generation can build, from the words of Scripture, a picture of God which is true to his self-revelation. How can we relate to a God we do not know? Immersing ourselves in Scripture to acquaint ourselves with it is thus immensely helpful to personal renewal.

Kathy speaks of coming to terms with the sovereignty of God, and the theological concept that God rules as a divine and absolute authority, and oversees the universe he has created. Every Christian must grapple with the reality of this theology. Tozer says,

> God's sovereignty is the attribute by which he rules his entire creation, and to be sovereign God must be all-knowing, all-powerful, and absolutely free . . . The sovereignty of God is a fact well established in the Scriptures and declared aloud by the logic of truth.[2]

We must understand that God has decreed man free to choose and has given him a moral responsibility for that choice. By his sovereignty, he has also ordained that man's choice for evil will not derail God's plan for good for his creation.

Christ came into our wounded world to partake of our brokenness. As we press into his pierced hands the pain we have experienced because of the evil choices of others, we undergo an amazing, divine alchemy in which the evil is transformed into goodness.

It was that way for Joseph, betrayed and sold by his own brothers. Years later, after rejection and temptation and imprisonment and abandonment, after refusing to succumb to the seductions of money, sex, and power, he became the chief advisor to Pharaoh, the second in command of the land of Egypt. Facing his own brothers who had come to beg for food to sustain their families during desperate famine, he would finally say, "You intended to harm me, but God intended it for good . . . it was not you who sent me here, but God" (Genesis 45:8; 50:20, NIV).

These words are like Kathy's amazing comments, "I'm not even sorry that it happened because I have seen the grace of God in a marvelous way . . . I don't know if I would undo the past if I could."

In both Joseph's and Kathy's lives something miraculous happened. When God redeems pain and uses healed scars, he shows himself as he really is. Even the memory of past abuse can be used by God as a tool for the healing of others. History is full of the testimonies of Josephs and Kathys who have discovered the real God.

Without going into complex theological explanations, let me suggest a beginning place in this journey to discover the true nature of a real God.

Learning about God through Christ

God has revealed himself in words; he has also revealed himself in a person, Christ. Christ lived out his Father's original plan for what the human was designed to be; he showed us in flesh the divine image. "No one has ever seen God, but God the One and Only (the only begotten Son) who is at the Father's side, has made him known" (John 1:18, with NIV marginal reading inserted in parentheses).

Christ is the ultimate man.

I can understand why women who have been hurt by men want to relate to a feminized God; but this is a serious mistake. It is man—man as God intended man to be—who brings enormous healing to the woman who can learn to relate to him. It is a holy and trustworthy heavenly Father (one who does not creep into the room at night, who does not coerce perverted activity, whose footsteps don't sound in the hallway), a Father who encourages her growth at every point—physical, spiritual, mental, and social.

Certainly God transcends the human categories of "male" and "female;" yet we must not fall into the error of the radical feminist theologians who urge us to call God "Father/Mother" and who generally seek to remove the masculine names for God from Scripture and liturgy, or who seek to create an all-encompassing non-gender pronoun to describe him. All of this does not so much feminize God as depersonalize him. As the attempt is made to create an androgynous model, contact with God's intimate personality is lost.

God has revealed himself to us as a Person. Although sometimes using feminine descriptions of himself (Christ said he was like a mother hen who would have gathered her chicks under her wings), he has declared his personhood in terms which are overwhelmingly masculine. Even when looking at the meanings in the original languages and changing the masculine usage in cases that are generic in meaning or may have been misunderstood by prejudiced male scribes, there is still an unmistakable masculinity about God. We are invited to relate to him as Father, as Lover, as Husband. So we need to understand that in God divine maleness coheres peacefully and compatibly with divine femaleness.

Rather than changing the vocabulary of the Bible, we need to rethink our views of what maleness is all about so that we are able to relate to God through the powerful verbal metaphors by which he has pictured himself for us.

The place to begin this journey is with the male Christ who is a man unlike any other.

A friend told me of a journey to the far east.

The Buddhist monks surprised me. They grabbed their robes away from women in public places lest they be defiled. We couldn't hand them anything directly but had to pass it first to a mediary or place an object on the ground. Our training manual insisted: Don't sit on the same seat of a bus where the monks sit. A monk cannot sit next to you. In sharing a taxi upcountry, there must be a male sitting between you and a monk. Make it easy for monks to pass you in crowded areas, holding your skirt close to your body if necessary. It made me feel positively unclean.

When I encounter the misogyny (hatred of women) of certain vengeful mullahs and males with similar attitudes in our western religious holy orders, my woman's heart is filled with fear. I think of Christ, another holy man, and of how he came into just such a male-dominated society and began to relate to women in ways unlike any other man had related to them. Christ had created woman, he understood her, he had compassion on her, and he invited her to partake of his life and work.

The Gospel of Womanhood

The book of Luke has been called "The Gospel of Womanhood." His gospel opens with accounts of three remarkable women of faith: Elizabeth, who bears in her old age a child and raises him with such diligent care that Christ himself says, "no one born of woman was greater than John"; Mary, who submits to the overwhelming task of becoming mother to the promised Messiah, "Behold, I am the handmaid of the Lord; let it be to me according to your word"; and Anna, the eighty-four-year-old mystic who never left the temple, worshipping, fasting, and praying there night and day.

Having set the stage with these remarkable three, Luke continues to weave together the amazing variety and peculiarities of the people who populated the life of Christ. Women are not dominant in this study, but they are prominent. Christ's attitude toward them was chaste and tender and filled with consideration, a radical approach considering the culture of his time which decreed that women were unworthy to receive education, unable to function as legal witnesses, and worthless in contrast with their male peers. Actually, Jesus' open, brotherly attitude is still radical. There are few churchmen who can emulate Christ's purity toward women or his regard for them. Certainly, none can match his sacrifice. Listen to Luke. Learn more about Christ and his women friends through this historical writer.

Here comes the widow-woman. Her son is dead and she weeps, all alone in the world, with no one to support her, even her husband's family name is dead. Christ has compassion on her and raises her son to life. Is there any group more overlooked in our society than the older widow?

Here comes the town whore, a common woman of the streets. Weeping, she dares to embrace his feet. She washes them with her tears and wipes them dry with her hair. The company of self-righteous, indignant dignitaries look on askance. What does Christ do with this prostitute? He accepts her weeping adoration. Her tears do not embarrass him. He refuses to humiliate her before the shocked onlookers. He forgives her sins. One of the highest suicide rates in our society is among prostitutes. Christ does not repulse these women but turns toward them in compassion.

Christ lovingly heals Peter's mother-in-law. I can't imagine him cracking a mother-in-law joke.

Who are these who travel with him from town to town and bake his bread? Who are these who through their husbands' business contacts or wealth advance his public ministry? Aren't these the neurotic middle-aged women, with their emotional and psychological disorders—Joanna, Susanna, Magdalene, and many other nameless women whom Luke describes?

Here comes a woman with a "female disease." She says she has had a flow of blood for twelve years and her condition has made her

---

Something You Can Do Right Now
Go to Luke. There is an old meditative form called Christic meditation that is practiced by looking deeply into a scriptural passage and interacting with the Christ revealed in that passage.

Walk into the event as though you were actually present. See the setting, the sea, the people, the little towns, the temple pavement. Now move yourself into the historical scriptural setting, taking all your needs into that event involving the Lord.

For instance, turn to Luke 8:40 where the account of the healing of the woman with an issue of blood is recorded. Can you understand her fearful hesitancy? her desperation? Do you know what it is like to be unclean? What was she thinking? What would you think? In your mind, do what she did. Slip painfully into the crowd, touch the fringe of his garment. See Christ in that event, a young man, a temple pariah, levitically unclean. Some doctors speculated that her problem was psychological. Some treated her condition symptomatically. All gladly accepted her payment of their fees. Now she touches the hem of Jesus' robe. She feels too unclean to dare to ask for or deserve his public attention. She is ashamed of her humiliating, malfunctioning woman's body. What if he turns on her as the other holy men have?

But Christ feels her tentative tug in the jostling crowd; he knows a seeker's touch. He makes her declare before all the people that she has been healed. No more rumor or innuendo here—she has been healed! In front of the townsfolk who have unsympathetically misunderstood her condition, he calls her "daughter" and publicly commends her faith and sends her away with his blessing of peace.

What a man this is!

Christ alludes to women in his teaching. His parables and real-life encounters are full of female prototypes—the importunate widow, the housewife who has lost one of her ten coins, the widow who places everything she has in the treasury—an example to stingy, wealthy givers. He refers to historical women as sermon illustrations—Lot's wife, a negative illustration, and the Queen of the South, a positive example of faith. He becomes women's advocate by insisting that a man is not to divorce his wife and take another; he is angry at men's

---

mobbed by needy people, already on his way to heal a dying child, led on by a distraught father—but he takes time to search for you. What does he ask of you and what do you answer?

Work your way unhurriedly through the whole gospel of Luke. The Holy Spirit will use these Scriptures to surprise you with the living reality of a Christ who understands what it means to be a woman, a damaged woman, and who reaches out in love from almost every page, and who can reach from that powerful past into the present in such a way that the past becomes the present, and you are the one with uncleanness, the harlotry, the fever, the terminal illness, the unbearable grief, the loss, the mourning. He will not neglect you; he will not abandon you; he will never abuse you, or humiliate you.

capricious power and the degradation of women. He is the champion of women who suffer from such abandonment and rejection.

Even on the Via Dolorosa, bleeding and wounded, he stops to sympathize with the women who are weeping for him: "Daughters of Jerusalem, do not weep for me, but weep for yourselves and for your children . . ." He knows the terrible future of loss and destruction, rape and pillage which are in store for them all.

Luke records the women who watch at the crucifixion. He tells us that it was to these faithful ones, still attempting to minister to Jesus' mauled body with burial spices, that the glorious first message of Resurrection was delivered.

You must meet this Man Christ!

One of my favorite passages about Christ is Mark 3:31-35 (RSV). This again deals with Christ's relationship with women. "And his mother and brothers came; and standing outside they sent to him and called him. 'Your mother and brothers are outside, asking for you.' And he replied, 'Who are my mother and brothers?' And looking around on those who sat about him, he said, 'Here are my mother and brothers! Whoever does the will of God is my brother, and sister, and mother.' "

There are many times when I've thought of Christ as my Older Brother who regards me with respect, one to whom I can turn when some of my human brothers in the church batter me with misguided theology. I often go to this Scripture, place myself in the event, and say, "Lord, I have tried to do the will of God . . ." I have heard him speak from the pages to my heart, "My little sister . . ."

Renewing the mind with a knowledge of the true God as he really is may be the most exciting journey into wholeness you will ever take. Again, write down the things you learn, the inner thoughts guided by the Holy Spirit, the changes that occur. Miraculously, one day you too may be able to say with Joseph and with Kathy, "You intended it to harm me; but God intended it for good, to accomplish what is now being done, the saving of many lives."

9

Self-Forgiveness, Self-Acceptance

Kathy's Story:

With my ongoing quest for a deeper knowledge of God and the extensive healing I had received through forgiving and being forgiven, I experienced a period of euphoria which I thought would be mine forever. But then I again began to experience accusation and self-doubt. My past life made me very vulnerable to Satan. Even when you have settled it with God, the "accuser of the brethren" comes along and whispers doubts. How could God have forgiven you for all that?

I kept fighting back with teachings from the Word of God, but I finally realized that some things had been dealt with only on a surface level, and I was in need of a deeper healing than I had yet known.

I had forgiven my abuser. I knew God had forgiven me. But there was one important aspect that I had overlooked. *I had not genuinely forgiven myself.* You hear so much about accepting God's forgiveness and letting God help you forgive the other individual—but not too much is said about forgiving yourself.

What I decided to do was this: I asked my prayer partner if she would work with me on this new, deeper level of healing I needed. We decided to go back through each circumstance of my life and work through childhood memories that were still painful.

Prior to five years ago, there was little I could even recall. But beginning with my molestation, we went prayerfully back to the very first circumstance involving my uncle and myself. Just to get to where I could face that event, we had to spend five or six afternoons in prayer together. With each incident I remembered, I re-entered the situation and told the Lord what I was feeling. Then I asked him to forgive me for any feelings in me that were wrong. I also asked God to forgive the other person involved with me. And then, before God, I announced, as we completed praying through each scene, "And I forgive myself."

I asked the Lord by his Holy Spirit to reveal memories that needed healing. Many times I actually felt within my body the physical reactions of that long-ago moment. It was a painful process, but very worthwhile. And even though I had already forgiven in the broad sense, I felt the need to give and receive forgiveness with a witness for each remembered incident.

After each scene had been revisited and I had said, "God forgive him. God forgive me. I forgive myself. On the basis of your Word (1 John 1:9), I claim that you have faithfully and justly forgiven and cleansed me," I would then go on to the next circumstance and do exactly the same thing. With every young man that I could remember being with, I confessed my sin and again claimed 1 John 1:9. My prayer partner and I worked through my life right up to that very day.

Now, with a witness to my confession, I laid claim to God's promise of complete pardon and cleansing. I suddenly found I had strengthened my defense against the accuser. Now, when I sensed accusation, I could say, "I have dealt with that before God. I have dealt with that before my sister in Christ. She is my witness. And God is my witness. You have no basis on which to bring me into judgment."

With this prayer work done, I could continue with what has been a long and slow process for me: learning to accept myself; learning, even, to *like* myself.

The abuse survivor moves into life with her self-worth really de-stroyed. That is something I still have to work on. Because I'd been violated as a person, I questioned everything about myself. When you've been used and abused, you feel you are of no worth to anybody—other than to be used. So self-acceptance has got to be one of the hardest struggles. Forgiving the abuser, learning to think straight about God—those things seem to come easier. But I have to continuously work on self-acceptance, reaffirming that I am a person of value and accepted before God.

You have to learn to see yourself as an individual created in the image of God, marred most certainly by sin, but still an individual created uniquely for God's special purposes.

It's a strange thing, but your husband can say, "I love you, I love you, I love you," and all you think is, "How could he love me?" It's not enough to live on another person's estimate of your worth — although I'm sure it helps. You've got to come to accept yourself.

✳ ✳ ✳

Perhaps the most difficult act of forgiving and the most critical one for the abuse survivor is learning to forgive herself. She must forgive herself with the same determination with which she forgives those who have brought her pain. A whole jury of self-accusations cries out against her: Why didn't I get help? Why didn't I say "No!"? Why did I com-pound my plight with acts of emotional self-mutilation? Why didn't I accept the truth sooner?—perhaps I could have salvaged my marriage, raised my children better? What is wrong with me? How can anyone stand me? How can I stand myself?

When I talk with victims of child abuse who now carry not only the displaced guilt of the truly guilty perpetrator but also struggle with the weighty baggage of self-hate, I remind them that they are a lot like the little child who was introduced to a dope habit early in life. Some adult injected a small dose of heroin into the child's vein, con-tinually increasing the dosage until a dependency had been created.

Of course the child enjoyed the drug-induced high, loved the effusive moments, craved other injections. Of course, the child now has to deal with the effects of that addiction, the insatiable need for more, the days lost to stupor, the cycle of physical and emotional highs and lows, the humiliating ugliness of withdrawal.

But the culpability, the true guilt, the error was on the part of that adult who stabbed the needle in the child's skin and injected the first dose, then the next, then the next. The child is not responsible for that adult's action.

Child sexual abuse is the same. You are struggling against the symptoms of withdrawal, from an act (or acts) perpetrated against you of which you were innocent—and there is a confusing welter of causes and consequences—but you were not guilty in that first act. This realization can become a foundation on which you can lay the other bricks of self-forgiveness.

Begin by saying aloud the words, "I forgive myself." Forgive yourself for the moments that were not your responsibility but for which you have held yourself in judgment. Deal in confession with those actions which are your responsibility: your hatred, resentment, and bitterness; your sinful lifestyle; your vindictive "taking it out" on the people around you.

Take some quiet time and write out the specifics: I confess and forgive myself for searching for love in promiscuity. I forgive myself for trying to punish my parents by experimenting with drugs. I forgive myself for my hatred toward my husband who was innocent of the crimes which were really the crimes of my father. I forgive myself. I forgive.

The release this kind of forgiveness provides is indescribable to those who have never experienced it; it is like laying down the ten-pound load of pain strapped to your chest which you have carried to bed, through each day, to work, into all your relationships. You put it down, truly lay it aside when you forgive yourself. Then you can rejoin the dance of life.

Accepting Ourselves

I am still searching for an acceptable answer to the question: "Why? Why me? What is it about me that seems to elicit abusive treatment from men?" I can believe that at this point there may be characteristics in my personality that encourage an abusive relationship. But I cannot and will not believe that at the age of ten, I elicited this type of behavior . . .

* ✳ *

I was abused sexually as a child from about ages seven to fifteen . . . I heard someone say something about how a person stops growing emotionally when this happens. I think that happened to me because I have found that I am an emotional cripple. Emotionally, I am still seven years old.

* ✳ *

. . . for some time now I've been asking for the Lord to show me why I am such a low achiever. I know it's because I set my standards very low, but why do I do that? I know I can achieve, but it seems like I don't want to . . . or [feel I] shouldn't?

* ✳ *

I was a victim of sexual abuse. I have very low self-esteem. It took me a long, long time to figure out that I was worth something.

* ✳ *

Feelings of despair and hopelessness overwhelm me and I think people can see how dirty I really feel.

Clearly the survivor of child sexual abuse needs to think differently about herself if she is to really move into new life with confidence. The circumstances of her past have programmed her to feel dirty, worthless, and unlovable. Her response to these feelings may take many extremes: over- or under-achievement, promiscuity or ascetism, hiding herself in unattractive clothing or obesity, or flaunting herself sexually.

The balancing gyroscope at the center of an abuse victim's being which should help her establish and maintain her identity as a person and a woman has been knocked off center. She stands in a circle and turns and turns and turns; when she stops, she can't find her balance but gropes and weaves and stumbles. For the abuse survivor, this dizzy confusion may continue in one form or another for the rest of her life.

Her guilt, real or false, her damaged inner self-conception, all present her with a negative image which she actually reinforces by refusing to accept positive information about herself and by virtually collecting data to verify her negative hypothesis about her own worth.

Rebuilding self-image that has been shattered is an arduous journey in learning to: 1) refuse the effects of the past; 2) nurture and even parent oneself in the present; and 3) achieve in ways that will provide esteem milestones for the future. This is no insignificant task.

The abuse survivor has learned to believe lies about herself. She has often swallowed them whole. She is like a beautiful hand-woven basket filled with slips of paper on which are written only negative comments like: "You're a dirty slut." "You can't do anything right." "You're worn and can never be mended." "You're evil." "You're ugly." "No one loves you." "You can't love anyone." "Why don't you just get rid of yourself. Everyone would be better off without you." These negatives keep whispering from her past and she complicates her healing by negating herself. It's as though without realizing it, she sits down and writes out additional negative messages that she crams into the basket of her self-concept.

Some of these messages have actually been spoken by the significant people in her childhood. She is going to have to go back and ascertain who said what and then begin combating those inner memory tapes rather than reinforcing them.

Lack of positive verbal approval in a child's past leaves any one of us vulnerable; the parent who could never say anything good, or who always held up an unachievable goal, leaves us prone to a failure complex, workaholism, fears of success, deprivation neuroses, and also leaves us unnurtured and extremely vulnerable. When this vacuum is complicated by a sexual abuse incident, particularly by long involvement in incestuous sex, the task of healing is enormous.

Learning to Be Your Own Parent
One thing we can do for ourselves is begin to be parent to the child within us. Your whole past lives within your memory self as though

100

it happened yesterday. Though you may have hidden away the incidents, or you may have dealt with them to the best of your ability, the child of your past, the young self you once were, often acts up in surprising ways in your present. I often ask friends to find that child within, to find her at a moment of pain, to describe what she looks like, how old she is, how she is acting. Then I ask, "Now, what does she need?"

"She is crying," someone will say. "She is seven (or eleven or fifteen). She is feeling alone and frightened. She needs someone to love her. She needs someone to tell her not to be afraid. She needs someone to tell her how pretty her new dress is and how well she jumps rope."

Once this kind of contact is made, the adult self can often begin to affirm, to nurture, and to comfort the child self. You simply find the inner child of the past and do for it what your parents were unable to do for you. In this sense, you can become your own mother. You can embrace and protect the child in your imagination. You can react in horror at the abuse. You can say, "It was not your fault. You did not cause this. You are not guilty."

Very often the therapist becomes a surrogate emotional parent during certain periods of therapeutic work. A pastor becomes a father substitute; a friend becomes a nurturing mother who cares, who is present, who says to us the words we have never heard but need so badly. The temptation in these relationships is to fixate on them because of past deprivation and to want to cling, to own, to hold. Skilled professionals will try to prevent this transference from getting stuck in the negative fashion; and those who are needy must teach themselves to recognize the relationships for what they are—gifts given for healing times rather than as permanent relational institutions.

Once the survivor of abuse begins to develop facility with Scripture, with prayer, and with knowing and experiencing who God really is, vast strides are made toward the healing of the broken self-image.

At this point the prayer of listening becomes a vital tool in differentiating between the negative image falsehoods of the past and the substitution of those lies with positive truths. We read Scripture, we work through Christic meditation, we journal our prayers, and then we say, "Lord, what do you have to say to me today?" and we listen.

Through the inner voice of his Holy Spirit, he often speaks powerfully to us regarding our damaged self-image.

A Special Love
One woman came to me after a meeting where I had led Christic meditation and she said, "I'm from an abused past and I heard the Lord say to me, 'You are my beloved.' Oh, I know he loves everyone best, but when I heard those words, I felt as if he loved me best, loved me in a special way and I had never, in my whole life, felt that way."

The miracle of this divine heavenly Father is that he has the ability to love *each one* of his children best! Such inner communications begin to heal the cracks of the shattered self.

We must get in touch with the negative thought patterns. Sit down one day and write out all the negative things that you think about yourself. Then one by one, take them to the Lord in prayer and say, "Is this true? Is this true? Is this true?" Then listen to what he speaks to your heart.

Catch the thoughts, "I can't stand myself. No one likes me." Chal-

---

Something You Can Do Right Now
Create a self-affirmation list. Take a clean sheet of paper and write your name—your whole name (or maybe a name you used for yourself when you were a child, a name you chose because your other name had too many painful associations—often victims choose a new name, or hear God whisper a new name as a symbol of their moving out of the shadowed terrain of their abusive past).

Now list under your name the positive things which you can honestly say about yourself. Number them and keep going while ideas come. Even if you can only come up with one good thing which you know about yourself, write it down. Reject, absolutely reject, any denial. Don't cross anything out. And don't write down anything negative. Deliberately hunt for items to add to this list. Your running total may look something like this:

Mary Sue Smith
1. I am kind, especially to small or hurt things.
2. I have a green thumb and help things grow.
3. I am courteous.
4. I have a nice nose.
5. I learn quickly.

lenge it with truth. "Some days I can't stand myself, but more and more I like what I am discovering. And furthermore, I do have friends. I will not believe this."

This is hard work, this self-correction, because the habit of negation has been insidious and lengthy. Often we have become so used to it we don't realize we're doing it. Make it a habit to tell yourself something good about yourself every day.

Now increase your abilities. Try one new thing you have never done before. Rent a car and travel somewhere; explore that unknown new place. Have friends over some afternoon for an old-fashioned English tea. Take up tennis or jogging. Write an article on an idea you have always wanted to explore and explain to others. Volunteer to be part of the office staff for a local political campaign. Plant an herb garden.

Each new adventure, each new ability we develop, gives us self-confidence, a feeling of accomplishment. Study Shakespeare; see some of his plays. Join a discussion group. Take a job in an area of work that interests you. These activities help us not only shake off our dark expressions but give us assurances for the future. We are building

---

You may want to get a friend to help you. Ask: "What are some of the things you like about me? I need to add them to my self-affirmation list." A husband can help enormously as well, but make sure he is prepared to communicate specifics. "I love you," though wonderful to hear, can become commonplace. You need to know that he loves to hear you laugh, that you make home a place of refuge, that he is intrigued by your ideas in conversations with friends—whatever. Take it all and add it to the list. You must not add mental disqualifiers to these comments. Just soak in the good stuff; let it sink in deep to the damaged self; repeat their words over and over, "Did you hear that, Mary Sue? Fred said he doesn't know another woman who could have handled that crisis with the children the way you handled it. He said he was proud of you."

In essence you are writing and slipping these pieces of paper affirmations into your basket. Affirmation is the rightful inheritance of every child. You deserve this after all you have suffered, after the self-doubt with which you have battled. This is what Scripture calls "edifying" oneself. It is a Christian activity. Do it as much as possible.

tomorrow's self-esteem by the inner journey and the achievements of today.

Especially if you have grown up in an atmosphere which has denied you good feelings about yourself, or where you have been demeaned by word or by action, you need to build yourself up through such honest self-assessment and affirm yourself through positive feedback. When someone commends you for a job well done, don't pass it off in your mind as, "She just says that because she's nice." You need that affirmation. Listen, believe it, tuck it in close to your heart. It is God speaking to you through the honest commendation of others. When a child says, "Mommy, I love you. You're beautiful," it's true! Believe it. Reach out and accept the daisies that are being handed to you.

The China Cup Can Be Made New
The abuse survivor may well feel like a lovely china teacup which has become chipped and broken, the imprint blurred, the handle lost. Badly patched, it has been stuck in the back of the cupboard. It needs the touch of a master craftsman—a craftsman like Otto. An immigrant from the old world, Otto's language was thickly accented, his shop

---

Something You Can Do Right Now
Here is a practical, workable plan for re-developing your thinking about yourself by bringing it into line with God's evaluation of you. Write each of the key Scriptures that follow on a piece of paper and tape each one up in turn on your most-used mirror for several weeks, so that when you look at your reflection, you will also see reflected back to you *how God sees you.*

When one verse has saturated your mind so that you can quote it, put up another. Over a period of time, you will gradually grow a new view of yourself—one not based on how others react to you, but one based on the eternal truth of what God has said about how he relates to you as one of his creatures. Ultimately, the worth of each of us resides not just in ourselves, but beyond ourselves—in God's estimate of us. Even when we feel "down on ourselves," this does not negate our real and great value.

1. We are valued by right of creation: Throughout Scripture, God makes it clear that he values people above all his other creations; that, having made man in his image, he loves and goes on loving all of his human sons and daughters.

   Meditate on and make these words your own: It is he who has made us

104

small and cluttered. But he could repair anything: the ornate molding that fell from old mirrors, the dimming paint of an original oil or broken china. He had the touch of a true artist, and when he had repaired something, it looked like new. He took great pride in his work of restoration.

God is such a Master Craftsman. With this difference: because he is the Creator he can make us truly new again.

When you understand your position before God as taught in Scripture, your self-esteem healing begins to take on rapid forward mobility. These truths can become experiential in your day-to-day view of yourself. See the section marked Something You Can Do Right Now for a structured plan for rethinking your self-worth. It is my suggestion that any person who feels that lack of self-esteem or negative self-concept is his/her particular problem, should begin to meditate on the Scriptures and other truths that are shared there.

Here's what happens: we find our self-identity by losing ourselves in his identity. Through this process, the tight knots of self-hatred and low self-esteem begin to be untied. We accept our worth as created persons, beautiful because of God's image in us. We accept the value—

---

and we are his; we are his people, and the sheep of his pasture (Psalm 100:3, NIV).

Made in God's image, made for his joy and for fellowship with him, we belong to God by right of creation, and he loves us with the special loves of the Creator for those he has designed.

2. We are valued by right of redemption: The fact that God loves us because he has made us takes on even larger implications when we see the meaning of the cross of our Lord Jesus Christ. For not only are we valued as creatures created by and for a king, our double value is demonstrated by the self-offering of Jesus Christ, "the just for the unjust, that he might bring us to God." Our low self-esteem may be exactly proportionate to our limited understanding of what God has said about us in Christ.

More words to think about and remember: This is how God showed his love among us: he sent his one and only Son into the world that we might live through him (1 John 4:9, NIV).

How much God values each of us can be seen most clearly in the price he was willing to pay to "buy us back" from the "dominion of darkness." As Paul says in Romans, "Where sin increased, grace increased all the more" (Romans the expensive price tag attached to us by the death of the Lord Jesus Christ for us. And we say, "Father, I accept your evaluation of who I am."

Then, as we accept Christ's Lordship, we allow his mind, his self, his love to begin forming itself within us. Ultimately, we renew our self-image not by focusing only on ourselves. That may be one of the real distinctives between a Christian path to healing and a secular one. We don't become aware of our self-worth merely by looking in, but rather by looking up.

5:20, NIV). Throughout Scripture this theme resonates: "But God commended his own love for us in this: while we were yet still sinners, Christ died for us (Romans 5:8, NIV). The cost of our redemption is a guarantee of God's incredible love.

God does not love us because we try hard—because we are good Christians—but because he made us for himself and found it worthwhile to buy us back from Satan and his dark kingdom.

3. We are valued because of the Beloved's acceptance: Paul takes great pains to teach, again and again, that we are accepted with God not because of our degree of goodness, but because of the perfect and wholly acceptable sacrifice of Christ. When we accept that sacrifice made on our behalf, we are fully identified with the Perfect One. These are big concepts. Because he sees us as part of this perfect Christ, God, who transcends time and process, already sees all that we will one day, in eternity, become.

More words to soak into your thinking: Dear friends, now we are children of God, and what we will be has not yet been made known. But we know that when he appears, we shall all be like him, for we shall see him as he is (1 John 3:2, NIV).

Rita

Rita is a winsome young woman in her mid-twenties, self-possessed, with an attractive shyness about her. Now a counselor at a sexual assault center, she speaks in a quiet voice about her experience of sexual abuse and her ongoing emergence from the long shadow it has cast over her life.

10

Understanding the Abuser

Rita's Story:

The primary sexual abuser in my life was my stepfather. But before my stepfather, I was abused by probably ten or twelve other relatives: cousins, uncles—you name it—from a very early age. The earliest incident I can recall was when I was about five, sitting on an older uncle's knee while he played under my dress. That started it; then there was fondling and later, with cousins much older than myself, full intercourse. It was always a part of my life.

When I was twelve my mother and father separated. Mom met another man, Gus, and we moved away from our hometown. Basically, it began with him paying a lot of attention to me, which was nice. I missed my Dad a lot. But my stepfather's attentions kept getting more and more intense. Within a year, we had begun to have intercourse, and this went on for five years. I was twelve when it all started and seventeen when it came to a sudden stop.

I found it all very confusing. I wasn't sure why it was happening to me, and I couldn't figure out why other people couldn't see what was going on. An alcoholic, Gus was a real con artist and seemed to be able to keep my mother deceived. A lot of the time I felt almost like "the other woman"—like Gus was cheating on mom and using me as the other woman.

I couldn't concentrate on school at all. I felt different from other kids and had no close friends. My mind was constantly on what was happening at home. I would get up in the morning wondering if it was going to happen that night, wondering if there was any way I could avoid being at home alone with Gus. I spent all my time preoccupied with the matter. I remember that my highest mark in seventh grade was forty-five, and I dropped out of school near the end of ninth grade.

Then one day I asked to go to a birthday party for a young cousin I liked a lot. Gus didn't want me to go—he never let me go anywhere. This time I decided I was going anyway. When I got home from the party about 10:30, all of my belongings—my bed, my dresser, my clothes, my bicycle, everything—were wrecked and thrown out in the middle of the street.

After this rampage, Gus had slit his wrists. Mom had found him and had taken him to the hospital. Then she and I worked frantically to get everything back into the house so that people wouldn't know what was happening.

I had a problem, though. I couldn't find my school books. When I went to school the following Monday, I still didn't have my books. My teacher, who lived two houses down from ours, walked from his desk to mine, and in full view of the class, put my books on my desk. His action made me feel frightened and exposed; obviously, he knew what had happened. Maybe everyone did. I never went back to school.

Now I just stayed at home. Gus worked out of town. He'd be gone for a week and home for a week. Those weeks when he was gone were heaven for me. I spent a lot of time hanging around with a cousin about my age, going to the hockey games that were the main entertainment in our small town. That's when I began to realize that I had a certain kind of control over boys and men, and I started using it. I

110

drank a lot, was very promiscuous, and just kind of hid the pain of my own deep confusion.

When Gus would come home, I would stay at home and be his good little girl. He never allowed me to have a boyfriend. I was never even allowed to look at a boy when he was around.

Everything finally came out when I met a young man—not really a boyfriend, but a brotherly kind of person who cared for me as a person and sensed that something was wrong. I had known him for a long time, but we had just begun to be special friends when, one night, we all arrived at the same dance. Mom was there, Gus was there, I was there, my friend was there. Part way through the evening, my friend came and asked me for a dance. Well, Gus was very protective of me. He just went snakey, fighting my friend right there on the dance floor.

But my friend wasn't going to give up. Now he knew something was seriously wrong in Gus' relationship to me. He waited until Gus was out of town and then he came over to my place and asked me a lot of questions. Finally I told him what was happening. He got the whole story out of me. He went straight to my mom and told her, and then I went to the doctor. I had ended up getting venereal disease from Gus; why I had never gotten pregnant is more than I'll ever understand. Certainly Gus never took any precautions.

My friend phoned Gus and told him that he knew and said, "Look. Don't come back here." Shortly after that, Gus killed himself. I struggled between feelings of guilt for having indirectly caused his death and anger that he had gotten out of it so easily—leaving me to deal with all my pain.

* * *

"What kind of man would do a thing like that?" The question is one of the first that people ask when they finally bring themselves to acknowledge the horror of child sexual abuse. "What sort of man would betray a child's trust? What sort of man would harm his own daughter?"

Gus, the stepfather in Rita's story, is one kind of abuser—perhaps fitting quite closely the stereotype of the alcoholic, self-focused "con man." But there are other kinds. Listen to a victim's voice:

The man who molested me at age ten was—and is—a Christian, a family man, a pillar of the community and of the local church. I do know that we are to pray both for the defiled and for the defiler. They are both victims of defilement. They both need ministry. And the defilement is deep. It is spiritual defilement as well as physical and mental.

Dr. Roland Summit, Assistant Professor of Psychiatry at Harbor-UCLA Medical Center, identifies "traditional values" as characteristic of incestuous fathers. Here is some of what he says:

The most typical incest offender is seen by his children as rigid, stuffy and old-fashioned. He is likely to place a high value on the obedience of children and the subordination of women.

He may be sexually inhibited . . . and tends to project onto contemporary teenagers a rampant sexual preoccupation . . . Ironically, his distrust of his own impulses, his fearful anticipation of his daughter's sexual awakening, his need to take control of her most intimate needs, his inability to empathize with the feelings of women and children, and his inability to acknowledge and communicate unmet sexual needs within a mature relationship, all combine to make him exploit the very relationship he is determined to protect.

Several other conservative traits have been found to correlate with incest. A strong belief in individualism and self-sufficiency promote isolation from a protective network of parental surrogates which might otherwise challenge the father's possessiveness. The isolation is increased if the family has judgmental religious beliefs . . . that emphasize the dangers in associating with people outside the chosen circle . . .

. . . It should be recognized without question that the relatively high proportion of traditionalist offenders still constitutes a tiny fraction of all conservative families. At the same time, we must be prepared to recognize that the decent, God-fearing, law-abiding pillar of the community is at least as likely to have committed incest as is the alcoholic swinger down the block.[1]

In *The Broken Taboo*, Blair and Rita Justice profile the kind of abuser who may well be active in the church:

> Barbara's father exemplifies how people can compartmentalize their lives: He worked, he had friends, he went to church, he committed incest. Her dad became religious when she was five and began teaching Sunday School. Her mother also taught . . .[2]

In the article "Intrafamilial Child Sexual Abuse in the Christian Home," Dr. Richard Butman discusses some of the factors which may contribute to the prevalence of incest in Christian families and the attitudes Christians should take toward offenders (see below).

As we go on to look at the characteristic profile of the abuser, we dare not dissociate ourselves from him. For we will find that he is not only our neighbor. He is very often our brother.

Profile of the Abuser

What is the nature of the child abuser? Recognizing that such offenders are not all alike, can we nonetheless form a composite profile? Studies suggest some common characteristics of child sexual abusers, and it

---

Intrafamilial Child Sexual Abuse in the Christian Home

Two factors contribute to the prevalence of incest in Christian families. Many religious families have difficulty dealing openly with matters of sexuality and intimacy. And these families have a tendency to have authoritarian leaders—the men in these families believe they "own" their women.

Just because a person has psychological problems (including incest) doesn't necessarily invalidate his or her Christianity. Such problems are painful reminders that we are fallen creatures in a fallen world. Although a Christian profession of faith should contribute to emotional well-being, it certainly does not guarantee psychological perfection. The harsh reality of sin in our lives should cause us to be humble.

When we profess faith in Jesus, we bring our raw material with us, including all our maladaptive habits (poor communication skills, limited control of our impulses, obsessional thinking). Although our motives and aspirations change, is worth our while to examine this information in order to achieve a clearer understanding of the dynamics of child sexual abuse and to find some answers to our horrified "Why's?".

With such information, we can move toward the action that needs to be taken:

—the personal act of forgiveness which sets us free to care;
—the family action of seeking counsel and legal redress;
—the corporate action of church discipline where applicable;
—the community action of prevention and rehabilitation.

Our primary interest in this book is in child molesters (within or outside the family) rather than in child rapists or others interested in "cruelty relationships" with children. So we will look primarily at the characteristics of what are sometimes termed "non-dangerous" sex offenders—those who are basically non-violent.

1. *Definition:* Researchers Nicholas Groth, William Hobson, and Thomas Gary offer this definition: A child molester is "a significantly older person whose conscious sexual interests and overt sexual behaviors are directed either partially or exclusively towards prepubertal children."[4] Such people are often referred to by the term "pedophile," which means "child-lover."

---

at least partially, it takes time for them to become firmly established, which is what Christian growth is all about. That's why the church—as a vehicle of teaching, social support, and grace—is so necessary in helping us channel these new motives and aspirations into significant personality change.

My own counseling experience has made me aware that Christians have all types of problems—including being locked into incestuous relationships. Learning to hate the sin but love the sinner is especially difficult with ICSA [Intrafamilial Child Sexual Abuse] because of the devastating consequences for all the family members involved. But since we can never tell what raw material a person brings to his conversion, we should avoid the temptation to judge. Rather, we should ponder the best way to manifest God's grace to him or her.
—*Dr. Richard Butman, Associate Professor of Psychology, Wheaton College. This material originally appeared in HIS, the student magazine of InterVarsity Christian Fellowship.*[3]

2. *Childhood background:* While child molesters show clear signs of inadequate socio-sexual maturation, the statistics do not show any particular relationship to observable childhood stress. According to a study by the Canadian Committee on Sexual Offenses Against Children, chaired by University of Toronto sociologist Robin Badgley, 90 percent of the "non-dangerous" sexual offenders came from structurally stable families with numerous siblings. Three-fifths of the 90 percent were involved in an adult heterosexual relationship at the time they committed the child sexual offense. Only one in five was a stranger to the child at the time.[5]

But although for many offenders there is no history of child sexual trauma, molesters often demonstrate childhood emotional deprivation which makes it difficult for them to form healthy adult relationships. This emotional scarring may stem from problems within the family or from lack of acceptance by peers during the growing-up years.

3. *Two basic types of molesters:* Groth, Hobson, and Gary identify two basic types of sexual offenders against children on the basis of their levels of socio-sexual maturation:

—Fixated Molester: This person demonstrates a compulsive and primary sexual preference for children. Male victims are primary targets. The persistent and compulsive behavior means that many children may be molested by one molester.

One study showed that homosexual and heterosexual pedophiles had an average of 30.6 and 62.4 victims, respectively—and on an average each molested two-thirds of his victims before he was first reported to the authorities.[6]

This fixation seems to be a result of inadequate resolution of maturation issues. The interest for sexual involvement with children is apparent from adolescence onwards, with the molester showing little or no interest in sexual contact with peers.

—Regressed Molester: This person successfully developed a primary sexual orientation to peers, but under some precipitating stress reverts to sexual contact with a child. Female children are primary targets, and the pedophilic sexual activity usually coexists with sexual involvement with a peer. This type of offender typically replaces a conflictual adult relationship with involvement with a child. In incestuous situations, the offender abandons his parental role, and reverts to adolescent behavior patterns, behaving "not so much as a grown man . . . [but as] a maladroit adolescent attempting to win a young girl in his first love affair."[7] This offender copes with life stresses by regressing to an earlier stage of development.

4. *Behavior in Vulnerable Relationships.* Any relationship of authority or trust with children is liable to be abused by a pedophile. "Step-fathers," according to Dr. Summit, "are five times more likely to molest a child in their care than natural fathers. Live-in boyfriends and transient suitors [of the mother] are also more predatory, on the average, than the natural father."[8]

In recent days, our newspapers have carried stories of foster parents, boy-scout leaders, reform school directors, security guards, school teachers—as well as parents—abusing the trust of children.

5. *Denial and Rationalization.* Many researchers point out that offenders who flout the taboo against sexual activity with children develop strong denial and rationalization mechanisms. When confronted, "a suspect is both passionate and often very convincing in his protests of innocence," says Dr. Summit.[9] Some may actually have developed a denial system to the point of amnesia. Karin Meiselman comments on this denial/rationalization syndrome:

> The incestuous father generally tries to alleviate his guilt and anxiety by reiterating . . . the rationalizations that he has been employing during the affair—his wife is frigid, his daughter is precociously developed and seductive, it is his duty to provide sex education, better him than another, and so forth. In trying to minimize the offense, he may insist that there was only "sex play" as opposed to intercourse . . .
>
> Some fathers react to the incest revelation with a strong denial of the offense . . . When this reaction occurs, the daughter is portrayed in the vilest of terms . . . If his wife wishes to continue their marriage, she joins him in repudiation of the daughter.[10]

6. *Marital Dissatisfaction.* Whether as part of the denial/rationalization process or as triggering stress, the abuser often expresses marital

dissatisfaction. He may feel his wife is cold, domineering, or indifferent. Although this dissatisfaction may be rooted in the abuser's own immaturity in a sexual relationship, he is most likely to project his problems onto his wife and claim inadequacy on her part.

7. *Precipitating Stress.* As with other forms of child abuse, child sexual abuse is deeply rooted in the insecurity and low self-esteem of the adult, and in his maladaptive ways of coping with life. And, as with other forms of child abuse, sexual abuse is often triggered by a particular stress (which the abuser may name as "the reason" in his self-justification and rationalization).

Wesley R. Monfalcone in *Coping with Abuse in the Family* names some of these triggering stress situations:

—financial crises including unemployment or business reversals;
—illness of a spouse, creating frustration and resentment;
—a feeling of being trapped by the circumstances of life;
—a non-supportive or absent spouse;
—alcohol and drug addiction.[11]

Summit sees that "the man most often seeks sexual contact with a child when he is frustrated in his usual adult gratifications. He may be out of work, disabled, passed over for promotion, or rejected in an attempted affair."[12]

8. *Need for Power and Control.* The real issue in sexual molestation is more one of power and control than one of sexuality. With a child, the adult perpetrator feels he can be the undisputed dominant partner. Religious views that allow a man to feel he has the right to absolute control over his wife and daughters may be used as justification.

Shirley O'Brien investigates the emotional level of the perpetrator and states, "The adult perpetrator is trying to find an extension of himself with the victim. That is, he is seeking narcissistic autoeroticism . . . Such an adult sees a relationship with a child as less threatening because in such a situation he does not feel inferior. He is in control."[13]

Most authorities agree that the child molester is arrested in his own psychological and emotional development. Louise Armstrong says,

"The abusive father must have a sense of paternalistic prerogative in order to even begin to rationalize what he's doing . . . Weak or authoritarian in nature, he must have a perception of his children as possessions, as objects. He must see his children as there to meet his needs—rather than the other way around."[14]

The majority of child molesters are not psychotic. Of course, there is a chilling minority who systematically prey on children with the intent to coerce, punish, torture, humiliate, and sometimes even maim and kill. These offenders, considered "dangerous" in the sense of being potentially violent, are very likely to have abuse backgrounds of their own.

Nicholas Groth reports in his book *Men Who Rape* that there was evidence of early sexual trauma in the life histories of about 33% of the offenders with whom he worked, a significantly greater percentage than the 10% incidence of sexual trauma reported by adult male non-offenders. Groth then notes: "The offender's adult crimes may be in part a repetition and acting out of a sexual offense he was subjected to as a child, a maladaptive effort to solve an unresolved early sexual trauma."[15]

Our Voices echo this researcher's words:

My husband was molested as a child. Then a few years ago he molested some little girls. He is emotionally abusive and my son and I hate the way he behaves when he is angry. There has been so much hurt and damage . . . and he still blames other people for things he did wrong.

* ✳ *

Yes, I too was abused as a child, but I had begun to believe my own rationalizations and would never admit even to myself that I was actually a molester.

The Badgley report found that 98 percent of the potentially violent offenders came from broken homes. These offenders, in contrast to the non-violent offenders, were rarely married, and most had previous criminal records. Three in four of the potentially violent offenders were strangers to the child at the time of the offense.[16]

Is There Any Justice?

A recent California study estimated that 95 percent of arrested child molesters do not go to prison. Of 30,000 child molesters in California in 1979, only 160 were jailed or hospitalized. Eight out of ten child molesters who are prosecuted are convicted, but nine out of ten child molesters are not prosecuted at all.[17]

Charges are often dismissed because the child molester is judged to be non-violent, or a first offender, or because the family drops the charges. Usually, the only witness is a child whom prosecutors tend to regard as unreliable. The pedophile has often intentionally picked victims who would make the least credible witness in the event of detection.

The Badgley report noted, with irony, that when fathers committed against their own children the same offenses that "dangerous offenders" committed against strangers, they were rarely convicted as dangerous offenders.[18] Judges did not consider an in-family offense to be as dangerous as one committed against a stranger's child.

One hears, hauntingly, the prophetic judgment of Isaiah:

So justice is driven back,
    and righteousness stands at a distance;
truth has stumbled in the streets,
    honesty cannot enter . . .
The Lord looked and was displeased
    that there was no justice.
He saw that there was no one,
    he was appalled that there was no one to intercede.
(Isaiah 59:14-16, NIV)

Pornography and Child Sexual Abuse

More and more studies are linking pornography to early child sexual offenders. Psychologist William Marshall at Kingston Penitentiary and Queens University recently found that seven out of a group of eighteen rapists studied who used 'consenting' pornography to instigate a sexual offense said that it provided a cue to elicit fantasies of forced sex. Similarly, ten of the eighteen who currently used 'consenting' sex stimuli, used it to elicit rape fantasies. He writes, "In fact, the one rapist who reported using child pornography as an incitor actually raped a fifteen-year-old girl on that occasion. This again reveals the capacity of various forms of pornography to elicit favored fantasies that may lead to crime."[19]

In his most recent study, Marshall found that almost half of the rapists he interviewed used so-called "soft core" consenting sex pornography to arouse themselves in preparation for seeking out a victim. 38 percent used consenting sex pornography immediately prior to committing an offense, and 19 percent of the rapists used forced-sex, sadistic-bondage pornography to incite them to rape. Even more strikingly, he found that 55 percent of homosexual child molesters he studied imitated child pornography in their crimes.[20]

I remember the things my father forced me to do and the disgusting magazines and books he kept hidden away.

∗ ✳ ∗

I would do anything to help stop the flood of pornography. My abuser regularly excited himself with it . . .

Can Incestuous Fathers and Other Child Molesters Be Helped?
The attitude of much of the professional psychological community has been: Once a pedophile, always a pedophile. Other experts state that help for the confirmed child molester, for the habitual incestuous father, is as difficult but no more difficult than that for the alcoholic—both are addicted to a habit beyond their control.

According to Alexander G. Zaphiris, a professional who has conducted intensive research into the causes and effects of incest, the best environment for healing is one in which professionals dealing with incestuous situations put aside their own revulsions and bring professional, diagnostic, and rehabilitative skills to their therapy; one in which the community (especially the law enforcement and the criminal justice systems) develops a non-punitive and collaborative cooperation;

one in which there is a unique treatment designed to include both the differences of individuals as well as the commonalities of incest; and a sufficient length of treatment (two to three years of weekly, one hour sessions) to ensure a comprehensive and permanent outcome.[21]

Can abusers be helped? Yes, they can. With extensive therapy and a caring community, they *can* move toward wholeness. But in order to help them, we need to enter their worlds and listen to their stories, just as we have listened to their victims'. We need to put aside our own personal revulsions about the *act* of child sexual abuse and look at the abuser as a *person*, a fellow human being. Healing takes work, cooperation, and time, as George's story in the next chapter will show.

George

I went to jail to meet George, a Christian man charged and found guilty of sexually abusing his daughters. Sitting across from him in a private office assigned to me for the interview, I found my horror and revulsion at the act of abuse gradually transformed into compassion for the offender. George was a broken man; a brokenhearted man. Not a big man, in jail he had a nervous manner. A light beard failed to hide the scars of acne on his face. He told me his story in the hope that it would help other offenders face their sin and move toward wholeness.

11
Portrait
of an
Abuser

George's Story:

I'm thirty-five now. I grew up in a relatively well-balanced family, believe it or not, although I was always closer to my mother than my father. My father was very distant emotionally, quite a disciplinarian but not very able to show love or affection. As I grew up, I was not accepted by girls of my age. Children, though, accepted me and didn't comment on my face or scorn me, so I felt accepted by them.

I came to know the Lord in my late teens through a young people's group. I gave my life to the Lord—although there were some problems that I still had. I continued in fellowship with the church, becoming a deacon by the time I was thirty-one. In outward appearance, I was a very good Christian, but inwardly I knew I had some serious problems. I continued to experience attraction to little girls.

I had married my wife when she had just turned eighteen. Our relationship was never really good. For my own part, I was playing roles; I appeared to be all together, but inside there were real problems and as time went on, the marriage broke down. At the time of our separation, my wife may have suspected something wrong in my relationship with our daughters, but she never really said anything. I don't think she knew that I had become incestuously involved with our daughters until a few months ago when I turned myself in to the police.

Our older daughter was about four or five when I started to caress her improperly. I knew what I was doing was wrong and yet I reasoned that it wasn't really me doing it—it was the devil in me, or whatever. Then I would say to myself, "Well, she doesn't mind it . . . she isn't saying anything . . . she isn't reacting . . . she isn't pulling away . . . so it's not that bad. Maybe she enjoyed it."

And yet I never thought it was right; I knew it was wrong and I enjoyed it. It is very hard to think about it now, but I did enjoy it. I would rationalize and say, "Well, God forgive me. I know what I did was wrong, but it won't happen again." Until the next time.

Something that I've learned in therapy is that the offender does not view incest as a problem. Like other abuse offenders, I thought of the intimate caressing in which I was indulging as a solution to the big problems I had: the lack of communication and affection from my wife, for instance, and my own lack of self-confidence. Some people would use alcohol as a solution. Incest was mine.

My oldest daughter was the one that I assaulted repeatedly. It is hard to think of it in those terms, but it is true. That is what I did. Although it was loving and gentle and caressing, it was still assault.

Then there were other children involved as well—family friends. One was four, and the other girls were between eight and ten years of age. One was the daughter of my best friend. I was trusted; I babysat the girls; I took care of them.

In September of this last year, I mentioned to my best friend the problems I was having with my own daughters. Though there had been a while in which I hadn't molested them, suddenly within the span of two weekends I molested two girls. I knew I couldn't go on like that. It was way out of control and I couldn't seem to stop it. But my pride was in the way. How could I go and talk to somebody about that? They would view me as some horrible monster.

I asked the Lord, "Just what can I do to stop this?" I didn't know what to do.

After this there was a rapid chain of events. On Tuesday morning, a couple of people phoned one of the elders and commented about my actions around young children—young girls—and the elder went and talked to my best friend to ask if he knew of any problem. My friend said, "Yes, there is a problem, but I don't know how advanced it is."

My friend then went home that day and asked his daughter how she felt about me, and she said, "He touched me" and then cried for ten minutes. She told him what had happened—that I had fondled her inside her panties. He prayed about what to do for two days before he confronted me. He wasn't sure what to do. Then the Lord led a couple of people to talk to him about their role in child abuse cases. On Friday he came to me and said, "Look, either you get help or I will file a complaint." The elders contacted me Friday afternoon and asked to meet with me Saturday morning. At that point, my whole house of cards collapsed around me.

I was still feeling very sorry for myself. Every incest offender feels like a victim of everything else, like it is somebody else's fault. So on Saturday, I went and talked to the elders and gave them a list of all the girls and told them in general terms what had happened.

It was still hard to deal in detail with what I did. I know what I did; I understand how far I went and how far I could have gone and that's why the help was needed. My daughters needed help, and I needed help because I knew that as they grew older, it would turn into intercourse.

So the elders contacted Social Services and I went over for an interview with them and told them about my daughters. I didn't tell them about the other girls. The elders contacted my wife (we had been separated for about a year and a half by that time) and told her what was going on.

At this point Social Services contacted the police and my minister did, too. I had no choice but to turn myself in. Then I was arrested and charged with sexual assault. I was allowed out on my own recognizance since they didn't feel I was a threat, but they did require a psychological assessment.

I was given a court date in October to go and face the charges, and in January I pleaded guilty. During the time from September to January I had been continuing treatment with forensic assessment and an incest offenders group therapy program which has really helped.

In therapy, they don't pull any punches; they tell it to you straight. The group members are there to work things out together and to say, "Look, you are giving us a snow job and you know it!" If you start lying, they know it, and they'll tell you. Psychologists and psychiatrists know the workings of the human mind and how the guards go up.

I know I need intensive treatment. You can't expect it to change in four months and then live happily ever after. It doesn't work like that. Incest doesn't go away by itself. You can pull the leaves off and cut it off at the stem, like staying away from children, from my daughters; but I can only do that for so long. Then, when we get back together, what is going to happen? I have to get treatment; there is no other way.

I was a pedophile. I still am. I have to understand that for the rest of my life, I am an incest offender—like the alcoholic who has not taken the drink but still is an alcoholic.

I have seen the damage in my girls when they cry, when they feel very uptight about what they are discussing in counseling. The damage that I caused is enough to stop me, and yet given the possibility of being with a twelve-year-old under certain conditions—well, I just don't trust myself.

I have verbally, or through letters, told all the girls—"I am responsible, you are not." That is the terrible thing with incest — the guilt. Because the physical feelings are all there, a child does feel good but knows it is wrong. Thus there is a lot of confusion. So the father must take the responsibility and say and believe, "I did it, and it was me that did it, and you had nothing to do with it. It is wrong and I shouldn't have done that."

The church is still dealing with this situation and finds it very hard. The church at large has been negligent about this problem, thinking, "It could never happen here." At the request of the elders, I told the congregation at a communion service what was happening, that I was guilty of improperly touching girls.

The elders at one point got together with me and said, "You are not

128

dealing with this. You say all the right things, but we don't see that anything has really changed. You are still manipulating, you are still trying to get people to accept you without change." They decided to withdraw church fellowship a week before I entered prison.

So on that Sunday I went to another church, and the minister, because of a problem with adultery within his congregation, preached on the difference between Godly sorrow and human sorrow. Godly sorrow is repentance; human or worldly sorrow is manipulation. God really spoke to me through that man—the truth hit me between the eyes. That Thursday in the incest group, we discussed my own view of what was going on and the fact that I wasn't really dealing with my problem except on an intellectual level.

That week everyone said, "Look, deal with it and let us know what is really going on inside." I was afraid because I still had these feelings for children and I knew it was wrong. I had not assaulted any child since the time of the arrest in September, but the feelings were still there.

It was very painful because I was still trying to hide, and in that therapy session before I was sentenced I did a lot of work in the group and got a lot of things out. I worked through and started to deal with my feelings. It was a time of reckoning, a time of getting to know what is inside me, and a time of just being humbled before the Lord.

So much happened all at once—the breaking of fellowship, the minister's sermon, the forcefulness of the therapy session, the sentencing when they read the charges before people in the courtroom and before the judge, the reading of what happened and how severe it was, the crashing of the prison doors, and the realization that I was here, in prison, because I broke the laws and sexually assaulted my own daughters.

God has used this to bring me to a point where I say, "Yes, I deserve to be here. I am the lowest of the low. I'm in with drug addicts and alcohol abusers; I'm in with people who are in for burglary and for assault—and yet even in this population, I am below them." This is not easy to take when pride has motivated so much of my life.

It has been very difficult for my church. I was very angry about the discipline at the time. Some people felt that it wasn't right to discipline me, yet it was very much what I needed. All the elders are good friends of mine; the church members are very good friends. I have known most of them for many years.

One thing that has to be understood about the incest offender—you can't let him off the hook, not for one instant. The sex offender wants to take the easy road. It is harder to communicate with his wife than with his daughters. It is harder to communicate with an authority figure or a friend. So he turns to the easy route.

But you can't feel sorry for him. He is the one who did it. He is the perpetrator. If they had let me off the hook, I would have continued. That is why the discipline has to be hard-line.

And it is very hard to be disciplined, to go through therapy, to go through a jail sentence. Yet that is what has to be done to be able to start straightening out. I say that with a lot of conviction because I have been there.

* ✳ *

In George's story, the reality of his crime was brought home to him by a church community that cared enough to discipline by, a brutally honest therapeutic exchange, and by sentencing and imprisonment. Without all of these, George might have gone to prison with his rationalizations intact, without coming to the point of saying, "I deserve to be here."

Drastic action does need to be taken. Removing the incestuous father from the home, providing immediate intensive counseling for those "defiled" as well as the "defiler," requiring confession to the church community, disciplining, then giving firm, practical extensions of love—all these methods are intervening actions which separate the offender from his perverted intentions.

I am currently in jail awaiting sentencing because I had sexual intercourse with my daughter. I have confessed my sins to the church and have been formally separated from the church. I now know the Lord can and does change people who truly submit and confess their sins. I have found out that I had friends who were friends indeed. There are many who have in Christian love stood by our sides and have given their time and means to help wherever they can.

The Church's Helping Role

The Christian community, when educated to the complex magnitude of the problem of child sexual abuse, can function as a healing unit to bring discipline, accountability, loving support, and a framework of true growth for the child sex-offender.

Historically, the church has been too timid in dealing with the sexual offender; too quick to proffer forgiveness without true repentance ("He said he was sorry, didn't he?"); too prone to support the family as a unit rather than the individuals within it. A family that fails to protect its own children is one which needs radical dismantling and rebuilding. Hasty attempts at reconciliation will probably only mean that the offense will happen again. And again.

Justice and Justice answer the question, "What should be said to the parents when incest is detected . . . ?" as follows:

—the parents need to know that the child is believed to be telling the truth, and even if not, the family has a serious problem that cannot be ignored.

—the parents should be told to get help and be guided in finding that help.

—where legal charges are involved, the parents need to be told the nature of those charges and what the consequences of those charges are likely to be. (In many states and provinces it is now required by law that any known incident of child abuse, including sexual abuse, be reported to the police.)

—the parents need to be told . . . that the incestuous behavior is not acceptable and must stop.[1]

Remembering the strong denials and well-worked out rationalizations of the child molester, church leaders must be wary of "quick confessions" which relieve the offender of guilt but do not mark a real about-face. True repentance is accompanied by a desire to change, a willingness to face and accept justice, a readiness to make amends to the family and to enter therapeutic counseling.

A genuine sorrow will result in a real acceptance of responsibility for both the crime committed and its long-term results in the life of the molested child or children. Even when the offender has been restored to communion, extreme wisdom must be exercised in restoring any ministry responsibilities in which temptation might be overpowering.

The church must become sensitive to the fact that *child molesters and incestuous fathers often are church members*. Once this reality is faced, the church must then become the community of healing. It must be concerned for the soul of the sufferer—the child as well as the adult perpetrator. It must intervene with spiritual authority, insist on truth, confession, on an intensive therapeutic process. It must forgive the offender and support the victim. It must love, support, supply physical means, hold the offender accountable for seeking health; it must nurture the victim, find restoration of lost innocence through Christ, and pray for the healing of memories.

The church must do this. What community on earth is equipped to do the job better?

12

The Mother of the Abused

Rita's Story:

The hardest thing I had to deal with was my anger and resentment at my mother. How could she not have known what was going on?

I remember that at one point we were visiting relatives in another town, and I was sleeping with Gus and Mom (believe it or not). He was fondling me in the night, and she got up to go to the bathroom. Apparently she had seen what was happening, although she never said anything the whole weekend we were there. She never talked to me. She never talked to him. But when we got back home, she blew up.

At first she was really mad at him, but he talked her out of it. He conned her into believing that I had seduced him. "We really should do something with the child," I heard him say to her. "She's becoming a real problem."

I was thirteen at the time. I can recall sitting on the couch, hearing them talk, and thinking, "How can she believe all of this? How can she believe him over me?"

Gus came out of the bedroom where they had been talking, very nonchalantly. (I remember he was just wearing his shorts. He was always walking around in his shorts; he never wore pants around the house.) And he sat on the couch beside me, put his arm around me and said, "I think maybe you should decide whether or not you are going to straighten out, or go to live with your father."

It just blew me away. My father is an alcoholic, and I didn't get along with his new wife. So I really couldn't go home to Dad. And although I didn't want to stay where I was, what other option did I really have?

So the relationship with Gus continued, although I think Mom chose to think it didn't. I never talked to my mother about it again, never trusted her again. Since she had taken his side once, I thought for sure that she would just blame me more for seducing him.

I knew nowhere outside my family to look for help, so I was effectively trapped in the situation. My mom used to escape to Bingo. She would go play Bingo to get away from Gus—and leave me with him. I would beg her to let me go, and he would talk her out of it. "She should stay home and do her homework," he would argue, or whatever. That was how he would get us alone.

Looking back, I realize she was what is called a collusive mother. She knew something was going on, but she couldn't have handled accepting it. Once I was in therapy, I was able to look at her situation a bit more objectively. I realize that our whole family is a very incestuous family. My mom got pregnant by being raped by her brother-in-law, for example. That same man went on to sexually abuse his own daughters for years and is now living with one by whom he has a child.

So I guess I understand now why she didn't react. She had her own past to deal with. But trying to build a relationship with her again has been the hardest task in my own recovery.

* ✳ *

In a little antique shop, an old print hangs in the window. It shows two young girls holding hands, dressed in pinafores, walking through the ancient streets of a European city, stepping in the sunlight. In the lower left-hand corner of the print a dark, twisted man-monster crouches, observing their every move.

The picture, old-fashioned as it is, represents every woman's, every mother's, deepest, most suppressed fear—that evil darkness may one day overtake the light-hearted innocence of the ones she loves most.

And yet, when the feared "monster" strikes, many mothers find themselves paralyzed—by their own crippling childhoods, perhaps; by societal expectations about building a "happy home"; even by biblical injunctions to submit to their husbands.

Mothers in incestuous situations generally fall into one of three categories:

1. *Passive/collusive mothers* who, by remaining passive about an incest situation, give silent consent; many of them have experienced child sexual abuse themselves.

2. *Unaware/unbelieving mothers* who cannot/will not believe the child's report, thus doing great damage to the child's trust as well as recovery potential.

3. *Shocked/grieved mothers* who are prepared to act on behalf of the child. These mothers give the child the best chance to recover.

Much has been written about the victim of early childhood sexual abuse; many studies are being conducted on the male abuser, but the mother (in cases of incest, referred to as *the non-offending spouse)* often has to deal with an overwhelming array of emotions, a maelstrom that threatens to blow her world apart. The worst has happened. Now what is she to do?

My daughter was sexually abused as a child and has gone from one crisis situation to another, never really finding any happiness . . . I cried and cried and all I could think of was the molester and that he had left my child an emotional cripple.

* ✳ *

I am particularly discouraged by the total lack of any help, discussions, or even effects of the revelation of sexual abuse on the mother of the abused, the wife of the abuser. I am both of these . . .

* ❋ *

I have not been able to find help for the mother of the victim.

* ❋ *

The mother and the wife is also a victim. I have suffered tremendously in the last years.

The mother's role in cases of early child sexual abuse is pivotal—how she responds, how she handles conversations about the incident or incidents, and what type of comfort and support she gives to the victim, her child.

Parents must understand that a young child has barely enough language to describe sexual assault in a way that adults can understand; so parents must be careful listeners without slipping into paranoid suspicion. One Voice says, "Because we lived in the city while I grew up, my mother warned me about males who might attempt to take advantage of little girls. I was asked to reveal to her any incidents of this nature. But when the paperboy was verbally suggestive, I never dreamed of sharing this with my mother. I was too embarrassed because I sensed that she would be embarrassed."

Sympathetic communication in a family should make talk on sexual topics easier; but in all these incidents there seems to be such an inward moral taboo—somehow the heart knows these hidden, secret actions are wrong—that open communication is not always easy, particularly between parent and child.

How to Listen to Your Child
The parent must be very careful to pick up on the communication attempts of the child whose verbal ability is inadequate. A child might say, "I don't like Danny (a neighbor boy); he's dirty."

Instead of the usual parental moralizing, "Oh, no. Danny's not dirty. He's a nice boy," which immediately signals that the adult is not open to further conversation, it would be wiser in all cases to inquire, "That's interesting. Why do you think Danny is dirty?" Then hold your breath and listen.

If the child says, "Danny pulled down Sandy's jeans," it is time to proceed with caution. Often a child will test parental waters of reaction by revealing incidents about *other* children (the same way a fearful adult will tell a counselor about the problem of a "friend"). "That's not very nice is it? I can see why you think Danny is dirty. Did he do anything else to Sandy?" It is to be hoped the child, in this moment of tenuous revelation, will feel that she has a wise parental confidante, that she is loved, that nothing she has to say is so traumatic it cannot be handled by a calm, confident authority.

Very often parents don't pick up the cues because the shadow hanging in their own subconscious mind is so terrifying. One must keep in mind that the victim of sexual abuse is most often pressured into secrecy about the sexual activity by the abuser, leaving the child feeling helpless and guilty with no place to turn for help and no acceptable way out. But there are very real physical indicators to look for:

—a child's clothing appears stained, torn, or bloody.
—a child reports pain, itching, bruises, or bleeding in the genital area.
—the child is diagnosed as having a sexually-transmitted disease of eyes, mouth, genitalia, and/or anus, or is found to be pregnant.

Some behavior indicators might be:

—Abrupt changes in behavior—sudden periods of quiet or depression, unusual belligerence or disobedience—any extremes that are not usual to the child's personality.
—Teachers pointing out unusual behavior patterns which have not been noticed at home. Children often "act out" a problem on the playground or in the classroom.
—An air of secrecy, hiding sexual material, or being vague about whereabouts or activities.
—Using language or terms to describe the body, sex acts, or sexual deviations which are not appropriate to the child's age or experience.
—Obsessive talk about a person known or unknown to the family,

137

or sudden, unreasonable intolerance of such a person.

—The unexplained appearance of gifts or material goods not given by members of the family.

What to Do with Your Anger

Without doubt, one of the most stressful moments is the moment when an adult learns that his or her child has been the victim of sexual molestation; but at this moment, no matter how overwhelming the feelings of the adult, it is the child who must have the primary consideration. The best reaction is to demonstrate a slow, cautious concern. Expressed rage and anger may frighten the already frightened child, and such outbursts from the parent need to be qualified, "I'm sorry I upset you. I am very angry, but I am not angry with you. I'm angry at the person who did this to you." A victim of child sexual abuse often feels personally at fault, so the parent must be very careful not to cast blame with questions such as "Why weren't you more careful? How many times have I told you not to play in the park after dinner?" etc.

If you sense that a child has made a tentative confession such as "he played with me," some gentle encouragers to further revelation might be "Can you tell me what happened? How did he play with (touch, hold) you? Take as much time as you want. Use your own

---

Ten Messages for the Child

Ten suggestions are made in the book *We Can! Combat Child Sexual Abuse* for conveying important messages to the child either verbally or nonverbally. These are:

1. "It's o.k. to tell me about it."
2. "I believe you."
3. "You are safe with me."
4. "I am determined to put a stop to this."
5. "It's o.k. to feel . . ."
6. "It was not your fault."
7. "Some people take advantage of children."
8. "I'm sorry about what happened."
9. "I will help you."
10. "I care about you."[1]

words. Mommy (Daddy) will not be mad at you. I want to help you, and I love you."

A question often asked is whether or not the child victim of sexual abuse needs counseling. It often depends on the intensity of the event, the damage, what kind of trauma the child has experienced. Certainly, if unsettling symptoms persist several months to half a year after the disclosure, then the wise parent should seek professional guidance. Some symptoms might be lingering bad dreams, unusual fearfulness, bed-wetting, or any continuing drastic change in behavior patterns.

It is often the parents, rather than the child, who may benefit most by discussing their initial feelings and reactions with a trusted counselor. The parent is the child's safest harbor. And with perceptive guidance from a professional, the parent is often the one who can give the comfort, security, affection, and healing that the child needs.

Many psychotherapists suggest that even if all seems well, it is advisable for a girl raped in childhood to have the benefit of preventative therapy as she reaches adolescence. The teen years are fraught with emotional and psychological turmoil, and a therapeutic checkup at this time might ensure that these years will not be further complicated by the residual effects of an early traumatic sexual experience. This would be the time to ascertain whether effects remain and to help assure the teen that her future emotional and sexual relationships can be healthy and happy.

Incest—Its Effect on the Mother

The discovery of child molestation is a traumatic and stressful event in any family; but the discovery of incest is like stepping into the viper's nest.

The mother who has discovered that the abuser is her own husband, or the child's father or stepfather, finds her role excruciatingly compli-cated. There is a triad that begs her concern—her child, the victim; her husband, the betrayer; herself, the betrayed—not to mention the rest of the family. One casual glance at the damaging potentials can convince the most uninvolved bystander that the hazards are explosive enough to blow the family apart.

Second only to the victim herself, the mother of the victim suffers the most profound emotional upheaval. Her immediate reaction is one of shock. She may feel a gamut of emotions in rapid succession—repulsion so strong that it ventures on actual physical nausea; confusion as she is torn between a whirlwind of polar loyalties (to her child, to her husband whom she still loves); jealousy which is soon supplanted by a deep, bedrock conviction of failure; betrayal by both her husband and her daughter. All of this is further complicated by rage (if there is any emotional energy left for it); and always the nagging, continual feelings of guilt.

. . . And I was in shock; it was like a death finding out . . .

* * *

After a year I have so much anger it's terrible. Please pray that she will make it through her adult years without a breakdown.

* * *

I cannot tell you the years of worry and frustration I have endured since all that transpired. Even though I have forgiven, I suppose I'll never forget. My daughter continues to suffer.

* * *

. . . something whispered inside me, "he is molesting her," but how can one think such a thing about one's own husband? The guilt I bear for not paying attention to my instincts is overwhelming.

* * *

It seems as though I can spot these men on the street, office, anywhere I go—there is something in their eyes. I have never been able to trust another man since then . . .

* * *

Oh God, the guilt has been almost more than I could bear. I did not know.

And the mother experiences grief at the loss of her marital relationship—how can it ever be the same? How can she ever trust her husband again? Her security is shattered as well as her hopes for the future. She is also faced with possible financial uncertainty if he is arrested or the marriage is dissolved.

No woman under any other stress—death, severe illness—needs more support.

Her situation may be further complicated by a husband who denies his involvement, who blames the incident(s) on the "seductive" child. Consequently she is forced to choose between her spouse and her child; and if the marital relationship is already particularly unequal in power, if she is the unduly submissive/passive type of woman, or if the male is in any way abusive, she is faced with overwhelming emotional odds.

Researchers agree that at this moment, *the mother's support and belief in a child's revelation of incest is the most important element in the child's recovery.* With this knowledge, she may feel forced to jettison her marriage—a form of self-sacrifice terrible in its implication for her and the rest of her family.

Now she begins to cope with outside opinions: questioners who ask why she allowed it to happen, implying that she knew about the situation and simply ignored it. This is an opinion often shared by many of the victims themselves—"Mother is all-knowing. She knows when I lie and when I don't do my homework. How could she not know that Dad and I . . ."

Others may insist, "If you had sexually satisfied your husband, he wouldn't have turned to your daughter."

Of course, sometimes the mother is maladjusted—all too often a victim of abuse or incest herself. In many incestuous families, she has become passive and, like Rita's mother, allows something to happen which is too big for her to handle. In these situations, there is often a mother/daughter role reversal with the adult becoming dependent upon the child or absenting herself because of work, emotional unresponsiveness or illness. When this happens, the daughter functions as the wife-surrogate, child/mother to the mother/child.

This role reversal deprives the daughter of utterly necessary maternal nurturing which helps her form a healthy opinion of her own female self. The sexual relationship with her father satisfies her underlying need for physical affection and closeness, putting her in a flip-flop power struggle; he has coerced and manipulated her and now she can emotionally blackmail him. She is also provided with a means of expressing her unconscious wishes of revenge against a mother who has psychologically abandoned her.

In one study, incest survivors examined many years after the affair indicated that anger at the mother was a serious problem in adult life. Of the daughters studied 40 percent continued to experience strong negative feelings toward their fathers, while the other 60 percent could be described as forgiving, although there were often problems with past resentments cropping up in the present. The opposite result was found with regard to the mothers—60 percent were definitely disliked by their daughters, while 40 percent were more positively regarded.[2]

An increasing number of observers, however, are beginning to find fault with the concept of the mother as a causative factor in incest. Sometimes mother negligence is involved; sometimes there is a passivity that amounts to collusion. But in many cases, this is not so. Louise Armstrong says,

> I hope that great care and thought is given to telling the mothers the ways in which what happened was not their fault. All wives and mothers have received a binding double message. As wives, we have been told our primary responsibility is to support our husband. To stick with him, to endorse his behavior, his decisions, through thick and thin. As mothers, we have been told our primary responsibility is to support our children. Can we blame women who, in crisis, are unable to decode this double message?[3]

Help for the Mother
What needs to be done for the mother?

The Nanaimo Rape Assault Center lists several helps for mothers in its book, *Realities of Child Sexual Abuse:*

1. The mother of an incest victim, especially at the time of disclosure, is suffering a major life trauma and will need massive support.

2. The mother may have requested help in the past, and may need help in counteracting negative messages of blame or disbelief.

3. The mother's need for support, reinforcement, and acceptance will continue for a lengthy period as she strives to deal with the emotional damage done to her and to her child.

4. The mother may require assistance with such everyday concerns as food and housing for herself and her children.

5. The mother may find herself in interaction with the legal, criminal justice and human resources systems. She needs information about their procedures, and emotional support when dealing with them.

6. The mother's traditional support systems may be disrupted as friends and family react in various ways to her situation. She may be under intense pressure from these people to refrain from taking any action against the offender. She needs support in the decisions she makes, whatever they may be.

7. The mother may fear for her emotional stability, as she undergoes the usual responses to her disrupted life. She needs reassurance that her reactions are expected and manageable.

8. The mother needs constant reiteration of these messages: "I believe you." "You are not the offender." "Your emotions are acceptable." "You and your child can recover."[4]

Every incestuous family should undergo thorough therapeutic counseling of some kind. Something has gone desperately wrong somewhere in their family. The pattern of abuse must be broken.

I've learned that more was wrong in my marriage than just the incest.

The victims—the child and the mother—both need help to recover. If at all possible, the family needs to have a chance to mend and find health. The perpetrator must be held accountable for his actions, forced to face his own devious immaturity, and then firmly led to a path of repentance and potential restoration.

It takes skilled professionals to juggle so many precariously balanced

143

pieces, but our Voices speak of hope.

I know God is working to heal the scars in her heart and mind. God still performs miracles; he did a miracle in our home. Praise the Lord forever.

13

Renewing
Relationships

Rita's Story:

I met my husband, Dave, before I left home. I was eighteen years old
and doing nothing, going nowhere. We got to know each other and
just kind of moved in together, marrying later on.

Well, we had a son, and things got really rough. Dave was from an
alcoholic home; I was from an alcoholic home. We were heading into
a very sick relationship. He needed somebody and I needed somebody.
The problem was, I needed somebody strong and he needed somebody
strong—and neither of us was strong.

Sex was a real problem for us. I had a very hard time with it. In
fact, I still do. I have a hard time giving myself fully. Even just going
to bed and going to sleep can be hard for me. I still find myself listening
for those hated footsteps of my stepfather down the hall. For a long
time, the only way I could get to sleep was to fantasize about a Prince
Charming who would come and hold me and that was all. Just hold

me, never ever want sex. And with that fantasy, I would finally get to sleep.

Flashbacks would constantly interrupt our lovemaking. I would have my eyes closed and when I would open them I would see Gus's face instead of Dave's. And suddenly I would push Dave away, unable to respond.

For me, making love was just a duty, something I felt I was supposed to do. I myself felt nothing. Absolutely nothing. At the same time, I wanted sex, because it was the only way in which I understood love to be expressed. So I got very good at pretending. Since therapy, I am able to be more honest and we are working things out. For example, if a flashback comes, I say, "I need some time, I'm having a problem." My husband is getting more and more understanding.

Another problem we faced was Dave's tendency to violence. He never hurt me, but he could really damage furniture. While he was growing up, his father was a very violent alcoholic—the sort of man who used to shoot holes in the wall and shoot at his wife. The kids used to have to hide in the bush when their dad came home drunk. All of that affected Dave, of course.

While we were struggling with our relationship, my oldest brother met the Lord. An alcoholic and a drug addict, he was really delivered and began attending a Christian fellowship. My brother and I have always been good friends, and he just kept talking to me and talking and talking and talking—and finally I started to go with him.

I can remember sitting with him in church one Sunday night when an invitation was being given for people to come forward to make a commitment of their lives to Jesus Christ. As I thought, "Not me. I'm not going up there. No way am I going up there," it just seemed as if the Lord himself picked me up and took me up there. I found myself at the front—and that's when I prayed and invited Jesus into my life.

After I found the Lord—or should I say, after the Lord found me—Dave started to see little changes in me as he had seen big changes in my brother. At about the same time, his father also had a spiritual awakening, and it seemed like all around us there were people coming to the Lord.

Dave has made a commitment to Christ, but he still has a lot of problems. He is a depressive person with very little sense of self-worth. He has only a sixth-grade education, and he's ashamed and afraid to talk with anybody—even a counselor. He still has a bad temper. At the snap of a finger, he can explode into a violent rage. But he is working on it. He even gets up every morning and goes to the church for prayer services. He is a lot more open in sharing with me now, and the more we talk, the better it gets.

Of course, we still have lots of problems to work out. But I know if it wasn't for the Lord, we wouldn't be together at all.

Difficulty in relationships is often a symptom of a background of abuse, but the symptoms form differing patterns. One person may seem socially poised, but keep people distant; their poised control raises a subtle sign reading: *Private Territory/Do Not Enter.* Others may be withdrawn, even anti-social. But both are equally threatened by the intimacy of real friendship.

✳ ✸ ✳

I want so much to be a good wife and mother . . . but I find myself off-balance a lot of the time.

✳ ✸ ✳

When my husband stands over me (before we have sex), I feel terrified, out of control, like I'm losing myself . . .

✳ ✸ ✳

I have really never wanted to let anyone get to know me. I've always wondered, "If they knew, what would they think?"

A psychiatrist reports, "Typically, patients with great difficulty in forming lasting relationships often have abuse backgrounds. A standard pattern is that of forming very intense relationships which they are then unable to sustain. Having set themselves up for rejection, they spend a lot of time experiencing the pain of rejection."[1]

Some may be able to think of human relationships only in sexual terms. They may become extremely possessive in relationships, developing a leechlike obsession with the other person that eventually

147

drives the sought-for friend away. Or they may be unable to make any lasting attachments because of deep insecurity.

New Parental Models Are Needed
In addition, in incestuous families where the father has been the perpetrator and the mother has been passive/collusive, emotionally distant, or has chosen to disbelieve or blame the child, the whole modeling system by which a child forms his ideas of sex roles and adult behavior is disrupted. The victim finds great difficulty in forming healthy male and female relationships. Again, an effort-filled process of reconstruction is necessary.

Early child sexual abuse distorts the ability to perceive men as possible friends or as accessible adults worthy of trust. The flirt/freeze mentality described by many of the Voices we've heard intervenes. Men are viewed primarily in their sexual role and are believed to be "all out for the same thing." Some women have developed a first-strike style in human relationships, a "get-them-before-they-get-me" approach. The men in their lives must deal with a come-hither, flirtatious sexual invitation (issued either because of true desire, or unconscious patterned behavior), or a barely suppressed irrational antagonism.

Both styles are, of course, unhealthy, immature social realizations. The abuse survivor's situation is complicated when her "flirt/freeze" behavior is responded to with the male's own particular brand of anti-feminism, his own private source of hatred, his stereotypic idea system, his own bedrock belief that women are simply sexual objects to satisfy his own physical needs.

St. Paul's Standards for Relationships
Can there be any greater breakthrough in male/female relationships than the understanding of the Apostle Paul (often wrongly labeled a male chauvinist) who proclaimed: "There is neither Jew nor Greek, there is neither slave nor free, there is neither male nor female; for you are all one in Christ Jesus" (Galatians 4:28–29, RSV)?

Paul applies this scriptural truth even more specifically in his instructions to Timothy, where he sets the personal standards of behavior that a young leader should model in Christian community relationships between the sexes: "Do not rebuke an older man but exhort him as you would a father; treat younger men like brothers, older women like mothers, younger women like sisters, in all purity" (1 Timothy 5:1–2, RSV).

Paul's standard for Christian community is the standard of the healthy family.

What a relief it is to learn how to relate to others without a sexual agenda! While a wise and natural caution probably is in order in all male/female relationships because of the power of our sexuality to pull relationships toward physical expression; I still maintain a firm belief that learning to view men not as potential lovers but as potential brothers is the first step in freedom. (Some women involved in past sexual relationships with their brothers will have to go the extra effort of putting aside the old pain, of relating to men along the lines of what a brother should be.)

One married male friend admitted honestly to me, "There are many women I am attracted to sexually but once I have gotten to know them, the sexual attraction ceases, and we are able to develop mature, Christian male/female relationships." We need to understand that sexual attraction often diminishes as we deny its pre-emptive position and prayerfully push forward to relate together as humans before God, his children in his family.

Interestingly enough, when parents have been what parents should be, giving the nurture, the love, the affection, the affirmation that is every child's due, the ability to establish healthy non-sexualized brother/sister relationships is enhanced in the adult years.

In fact, many child psychologists are discovering that it is the loving father who helps both his male and female children feel good about their own sexuality. The most wonderful gift a father can give to a child is fond, affirmative, positive affection. If he says to his daughter, "You are so beautiful. I'm so proud that you're my little girl"; if he clearly enjoys her company, shows interest in her interests; if he hugs and smooches, cuddles and wrestles; if he verbally encourages her, he is filling the love-well from which she will draw in her adult years in order to be able to relate as a whole person, not as a needy object.

Avoid Overreaction!
The tragedy in all this discussion of sexual abuse would be for healthy fathers to become overly scrupulous and to cease loving their children in naturally exuberant, healthy ways. We need better and better fathers in the church, fathers who parent their own children well and also take a few others under their umbrella of cherished protection.

It may be more difficult for some people than for others to achieve the goal of non-sexualized brother/sister relationships. But it is nonetheless a goal toward which we can strive together. The church must constantly evaluate the ways in which it is teaching and exemplifying such relationships.

Unfortunately, much biblical exposition has emphasized a hierarchical male/female structure. This may, unintentionally, make it difficult for the abuse survivor to feel accepted, welcome, and safe within the caring, non-exploitive community which the church must be. Renewed efforts are needed to open doors into this sheltered society which is especially able to commit itself to the healing and growth of the wounded within it.

Woman to Woman
Strangely enough, it is often the male/female sexual attraction that destroys our sister-to-sister relationships. The joy of strong friendships with other women has been celebrated recently by feminist writers who pointed out that the competition between women for male attention is what often prohibits healthy inter-female relationships.

Euripides once said, "Woman is woman's greatest ally." We need to work to understand one another, to bear one another's burdens, to do unto others what we would have others do unto us, to be hospitable to each other—all Christian concepts.

While working with female patients, Sigmund Freud claimed (in *Studies on Hysteria*) that child sexual trauma was the cause of every case of hysteria. Later he rejected this theory because of the astonishing fact that children laid blame on perverse acts by the father. Incest couldn't be that frequent, he reasoned, and thus developed his explanation of this phenomenon as being due to female "oedipal" fantasies toward fathers which had no basis in reality.[2]

More recently, while Kinsey's massive report on modern sexuality acknowledged the reality of child sexual abuse, Kinsey himself did as much as he could to minimize its importance. Some 80 percent of the women who had experienced a childhood sexual approach by an adult reported to the Kinsey investigative team that they had been frightened and upset by these incidents. Kinsey belittled these reactions. He hastened to assure the public that children should not be upset by these experiences. If they were, he reasoned, this was not the fault of the sexual aggressor, but of prudish parents and teachers who caused the child to become hysterical.[3]

Rather than male professionals, it is women who have listened to women seriously. Female professionals since 1970 have been largely responsible for exposing the prevalence of sexual abuse and bringing it to public attention. And once educated about the incredible reality of early child sexual abuse, church women show an enormous capacity to be supportive.

One woman undergoing therapy suddenly began to get in touch with her traumatic memory of past abuse. She went through several months with nights shattered by dreams as the memories of past events surfaced. A small group of church friends took turns sleeping in her house, comforting and loving her family through this agonizing period, sharing homemaking responsibilities, and supporting her husband until the worst was over. Her therapist termed this burden-bearing "an ideal healing model."

The Church's Help
An article in the *Sunday School Counselor* on child abuse reiterates the importance of church involvement. Author Gene Smiley writes: "The church is ideally equipped to minister to families during times of extreme stress and emotional trauma. The acceptance, love, forgiveness, and support roles that are at the very heart of the church's message are exactly those required for proper remediation, healing and restoration of families who have been traumatized . . ."[4]

Christ, in his compassion for both men and women, intended for us to form a new society, a kingdom society on earth that modeled the kingdom society of heaven with little emphasis placed on sex roles, but much emphasis on doing the work of God. The church has the potential for creating this harmonious society in small, spirit-empowered communities here on earth.

True Peace—God's Peace

For instance, for the abuse survivor, the sacramental use of touch encouraged by Scripture and practiced by many liturgical churches ("greet one another with a holy kiss") has great potential for healing, for non-threatening physical impact. Imagine being embraced every Sunday, before every Eucharist, as men and women speak the words of Christ to each other: "Peace be unto you." To be touched, to be held, with no thought of sexuality intruding; to have the words spoken that lay to rest the war between the sexes, the alienation between humans, "Peace be unto you . . . God's peace" . . . can be incredible in its efficacy.

The bishop of a large Episcopalian diocese told of a time early in his ministry when he had been at odds with "an obnoxious curate." One day at Morning Prayer, they found that they were the only two in attendance. At a certain point in the service, the peace was passed. "As we embraced and spoke the peace, without words, our animosities were dissolved and from that day our hostilities were ended." Can this not be a means to ending the hostilities between brothers and sisters in Christ?

Communion—The United Family

The movie *Places in the Heart* ends with a scene in a little country church where the congregation sings a hymn and partakes of Communion. Suddenly the heroine's dead husband is sitting there beside her, then the town racist beside the black man, then those who have been at enmity pass the cup and share the bread. In symbolic array, the filmmaker visually displays what happens to me every time I partake of this sacrament: I am brought into communion with Christ and with his body.

If you want your relationships restored, I encourage you to use the healing potential of these offices of the church. Before you partake of Communion, examine your heart: Whom do you still hate? Who still has the potential to wound you, either in real life or in memory? Take them to the altar in your mind (or invite them to sit beside you in the pew) and receive the elements with them, asking to be freed from their power, from the hatred, from the broken relationship. Pray for God's love to reach them at that moment in this unbroken Communion with Christ.

It is time, within the church, to nurture one another, to learn how to be brothers and sisters, in all purity.

Ministering Christ

The ministerial role, the priestly role, is also powerful. An ordained minister who understands that he/she ministers Christ can be an agent for healing redemption to the abused. A faithful priest *functioning* as a faithful priest can often shorten the therapeutic process. To make healing Communion available after therapy sessions in which the painful past has been invoked is an act of pure compassion; we are nourished and reminded again of the risen Christ through the bread and the cup.

If your church doesn't have a service for healing, find one that does. Ask for those hands to touch you in the name of Christ, for the oil to mark your forehead in the name of Christ, for the circle of protection to form around you in the name of Christ. Listen to the prayers, spontaneous or ancient, that human voices pray, often speaking on behalf of Christ. Place yourself in God's circle by learning to renew your relationships in the body of God.

These healing tools are available to us, but unfortunately the churches of my background—the evangelical congregations—have little understanding of their potential. And the liturgical churches, with their weekly enactment of sacrament, have often lost sight of the sacramental meaning—that God can touch us through holy moments, holy acts, holy hands. We need to rediscover their supernatural potential in our churches today for the sake of this needy, broken world and the people in it.

The body of Christ often gives us new mothers and new fathers. Paul writes about the familial responsibilities of the Christian commu-

153

nity, "Bid the older women . . . to teach what is good, and so train the young women to love their husbands and children . . ." (Titus 2:3–4, RSV). What a comfort for the survivor of abuse who is at a loss as to how to behave in human relationships! What potential for holy women to model what has been forfeited by the terrible past. The lonely one no longer has to go it alone. The victim does not have to be the victimizer. She can be taught to walk in a new way, freeing her children from the destructive patterns of her past.

In a courageous book titled *Out of Control! A Christian Parent's Victorious Struggle With Child Abuse,* K. Miller shares how she struggled to overcome child battering with her own small child. In the book, the author tells how she came to terms with her abusive anger partly through the women in a Bible study group who prayed for her and gave her good parenting advice, and partly through the help of an older Christian woman on whom she could call when the home situation got rough.[5]

Miller gives phone hotline numbers that parents can call when they are losing control or need help to break abusive patterns. But there is no reason why a local church cannot provide all of these assistances for members of their congregation, not to mention reaching into the community as a redemptive agency. Study groups that develop a philosophy of Christian parenting should be a part of every church's training curriculum. Older men and women who have been successful parents should be available to answer questions and to guide. Parents also need to find a person who will hold them accountable, provide emergency assistance, arrange to take the children out of the home when intervention is necessary, and intercede in prayer. These friends can help abusive parents learn to deal with unhealthy behavior and inappropriate anger in an adult way so that their homes can become Christ-centered.

The parent with a background of abuse does not need to abuse her own children. The cycle of anger, terrorization, rejection, and trauma can be broken.

The church can learn to listen and keep confidentiality, another priestlike capacity. Such a gift for the innocent survivor of a shame-filled past is welcome and comforting:

I'm not one to make friends easily. I select people who aren't gossipers, for these women can stone you to death.

Christ was the advocate of little children—"but whoever causes one of these little ones who believe in me to sin, it would be better for him to have a millstone fastened around his neck and to be drowned in the depth of the sea . . . See that you do not despise one of these little ones; for I tell you that in heaven their angels always behold the face of my Father who is in heaven . . . So it is not the will of my Father who is in heaven that one of these little ones should perish" (Matthew 18:5–6; 10–14, RSV).

He felt that way toward you when you were abused; he feels the same toward the child you are raising today. He is the same Christ who said, "Let the little children come unto me." He is the one who asked the men who harassed the woman who came to anoint his feet, "Let her alone; why do you trouble her?" (Mark 14:6, KJV). This Christ was familiar with abuse; he went through it himself. He was humiliated, stripped, and scourged, lifted up naked to die a brutal death. He knows what you have endured and what you are going through. He suffers with you.

But he also offers hope—hope that we can finally complete the journey toward healing. There is potential for the *renewal* of all relationships in the church; there is the potential for the *healing* of relationships within the church. Because this is the body of Christ, he can give us the right loves for each other, holy loves—loves that mirror his own forgiving love for us.

My healing started when I told my husband-to-be that I wasn't a virgin and I told him why. His response sounds in my ears as loud now as then. He said, "If you were a harlot, which you weren't, and the Lord had said 'She's the one,' you would have been as pure as driven snow." Those were wonderful healing words and I cried all my bitterness away.

* * *

My father abused me verbally, physically, and sexually. After years of struggle, I have finally finished my masters in counseling and am ready to help others. Recently someone asked me how in the world, with my background, I have become what I am. That set me to thinking. In high school, my church youth sponsors were a couple who believed in me, who loved me, who treated me as a part of their family. They were the ones who made all the difference in the world to me. I'm in my thirties now, and I haven't seen them for years. I found their phone number and just called—to thank them for their love.

14

The
Helpers

Rita's Story:

It was really the problems in my relationship with my husband that made me seek help. I blamed all my problems on the incest in my past. I blamed all his problems on the alcoholism in his family. I started seeing a counselor about the alcohol problem. And I noticed something: the more I talked, the better I felt.

The counseling center I was attending had a whole weekend seminar on alcoholism. Among the speakers was a psychologist who spoke about incest. I just started crying, trying to hide the tears so no one would see my response. I made the decision then, "I'm going to talk about this." So I went to see him after the session, and he referred me to an incest therapy group.

I was in an incest therapy group for six months. And during that time, I did a lot of work on my feelings about Mom. Being a mother myself helped. It became a matter of deciding whether we were going to carry on our relationship as it was—cold and distant—or whether

I could accept the way she was, the way she is, and the way she may always be, and love her anyhow. I feel I have been able to forgive her; and while I am still not really open with her, as open as I would like to be, we are getting closer.

Group therapy was so helpful for me that I went on and trained to become a group leader. As much as one-on-one counseling can do, it seems very important to be sitting with other women who are saying things that you don't know how to put into words. You find out that there are others who have experienced what you have. It ends the feeling of isolation, the feeling that nobody has gone through what I have gone through, felt what I feel.

The most important thing that therapy gave me was a sense of hope, the confidence that my incestuous past did not have to control my whole life. It helped me to come to a kind of acceptance of my past, and also to a point of taking responsibility for my future.

Let's face it. It happened. I still think of it. I still have the odd flashback, and an occasional flood of memories. Last summer, I visited a house that we had lived in with Gus, and I didn't think I could go in. But I went in, and it was really dramatic the way it unlocked frozen memories. It was, at the time, very painful. It took me a good week to get over it and to talk about it. But I think it freed me a little more.

I know that some people are nervous about secular counseling groups. But I think that God puts people in our paths to help us toward him. I have worked through a lot of things in the group that I still couldn't talk to my pastor about. Recently I heard a sermon about God being all the help you need. I think the church should stop and take a look before they put down secular counselors. I agree that you need God, but you also need people. God didn't take my problems away from me. He helped me. He put the right people in my life. He is healing my relationships, but I still have to work at it.

At my church, when I mention that I work at the Sexual Assault Center, people just sort of disappear. They don't ask what I do; they don't want to know what I do. I think that pastors and all Christians have to become aware that sexual abuse happens, and it happens even in Christian homes. Certainly there are a lot of Christians who have been affected in some way by sexual abuse. We've got to quit pretending the problems are not there and start encouraging people to get the help they need.

> I do need help . . . I heard someone say that a person like me or anyone who has been sexually abused as a child should have counseling for it. Why? If I am a Christian, can't I go to God for the healing I need? Or is a counselor part of God's provision in the healing process?

I heard Scott Peck, the well-known psychiatrist and author, say in a recent lecture that people need therapy when they get stuck, when they find they have reached a dead end in the ongoing process of maturation.

That is an excellent rule of thumb for abuse survivors as well as for those coping with the normal frustrations and abrasions of life. If we're stuck, if we realize we have been repeating a self-destructive action, thought, or experience, then we need to seek counseling. This can come from experts in many different fields. Spiritually mature friends can often give us wise psychological advice. Pastors and church friends often exercise spiritual gifts of discernment and knowledge that are uncannily correct and insightful.

The difficulty with the ruggedly individualistic John Wayne complex ("I can handle this by myself") is that it is often a smokescreen for plain old pride—a refusal to admit to ourselves or to the world that we have a problem, that we *can't* handle this by ourselves. While hundreds of people can testify that God himself met them at a point of desperate need, when they were utterly alone with no one to turn to, there are also thousands who testify that their spiritual, psychological, and emotional development was enhanced by others they trusted who held them accountable, who disciplined and encouraged them in their growth.

The human journey into maturation seems to be a rich accumulation of differing experiences—God alone in the desert places of our lives, the touch of other human hands lifting us when we have fallen, our own giving-out from experiences with God, and our giving-back some of the love we have received from others to those who also find themselves in desperate need.

We all get stuck in our developmental process. In fact, our human ability to create defense mechanisms that hide a painful truth from ourselves so that we can go on with our lives without having to deal with it is so efficient that a good counselor knows this is a major task: to help victims face the truth they have hidden deep inside them.

In the book *Vital Lies, Simple Truths: The Psychology of Self-Deception*, Daniel Goleman discusses the dynamics of our truth-filtering system. In order to avoid the pain with which we don't have the resources to cope, in order to avoid the panicky, humiliating anxiety created by circumstances beyond our control, our subconscious filters out the experience. This creates the proverbial blind spot, the mind actively shielding itself from anxiety, censoring information to provide a sense of security.[1] A major example of this for the abuse victim is the ability of the subconscious mind to choose to forget. Several of my close friends have, within the last years, had sudden surprising memories surface, memories of their incestuous pasts—all of which had been totally blocked from the conscious mind.

The counselor's work is to help us see through our own rationalizations, our denials, and our projections, our isolating of feelings from events, our selective repressions—much of which the healthy, truth-loving mind can do for itself.

However, when a human being has grown into adulthood without an emphasis on truth, without facing reality as it is rather than as he wishes it to be, without coming to terms with the natural bent to self-deception, self-awareness is much more difficult.

The survivors of child sexual abuse are often raised in an atmosphere of untruth, and consequently many have not achieved the resources for ongoing development. Emotional development has been severely disrupted, and victims often feel chained by their childhood circumstances. They feel they have nowhere to go, and nothing worth living for. When the abuse occurred during early childhood, the establishment of trust both in oneself and in others has been short-circuited. When the abuse has occurred during adolescence, social and relational skills are often arrested.

Approximately 20 percent of the victims who have faced early childhood molestations seem to show no long-range aftereffects. How wonderful that these don't seem to need help! However, in many cases of child sexual abuse, the ability to cope is so severely damaged that a good counselor is very often part of God's provision in the healing process.

Having been sexually abused by my father . . . you can imagine some of the difficulty that I've experienced throughout my life. For the past three years, I've been seeing a psychologist, and she has helped me tremendously to understand and change certain behaviors which may have resulted from this abuse. However, I must give credit where credit is due—that is to God, who is the source of all wisdom and healing. He has given me so much insight, and I am very thankful to him. I feel that I'm becoming more free all the time, but I really want to be a more effective Christian, not just a more effective human being. My psychologist is not a Christian, so it has been a little difficult to tie the mental, physical, and spiritual together in this process.

* ❋ *

Even though I thought I had "gotten over it" and no one else knew about it, the scars were there and it finally had to come out. I finally sought counseling with a Christian psychotherapist for marital difficulties . . . The counseling proved to be the turning point in my life. I was able to talk about the past and even in sessions with my husband to relate to him my experience. My husband was wonderful, and I worked through my anger and bitterness at my father which had carried over to my husband.

Real help can be found at two levels:

1. *Informal counseling*—through friends, others who have experienced and are recovering from abuse, and/or prayer partners. Preferably, such counsel should be sought from a sympathetic, mature person with some prior experience in helping abuse victims sort through their various concerns. An untrained person with a gift for asking astute questions which demand honest answers is also invaluable. A personal,

insistent why? can force victims to consider issues they normally refuse to recognize.

2. *Professional counseling*—therapists with various specialties can help through their overall understanding of the problems experienced by abuse victims. These might include:

—Sexual assault or crisis center counselors with specialized training and experience in post-assault psychological problems. They will often invite the person into a survivor's support group, one of the most effective means for dissipating the sense of aloneness which haunts many survivors. Many of the people behind the Voices gratefully point to these groups as vital in their initial steps toward healing.

Just this year, our Lord got me into therapy and into an incest group. For the first time, I am acknowledging the intense emotions that refuse to stay stuffed down, and I am wading through each memory: all that to say this: I need spiritual prayer and guidance.

—Pastoral counselors. Although in the past many pastors were inadequately prepared to deal with the specifics of sexual abuse consequences, a wise and discerning pastoral counselor with some training can have both the spiritual and psychological resources for helping the person who is dealing with abuse history. The pastor may also be able to provide a referral to psychologists or other trained counselors in the local area if in-depth therapy seems desirable.

Often, the professional minister can give enormous relief to the abuse survivor by using the valuable tools of professional services. As an authority figure and representative of Christ, the minister can hear private, confidential confession; administer Communion which, when offered as a sacrament, may bring healing and give comfort; perform the laying on of hands—all of which have significance for the victims of abuse.

—Psychologists. Specially trained in the dynamics of human interactions, psychologists are skilled in asking questions which will lead survivors into healing insights. Christian psychologists who integrate spiritual and scriptural elements are particularly beneficial to those who interpret life within a Christian frame of reference.

—Psychiatrists. Trained first in medicine, psychiatrists help severe personality disorders (which may be complicated by chemical or physical imbalances) or personality disintegration (which manifests itself in prolonged depression, schizophrenia, or psychosomatic illness). Sometimes a psychiatrist and a psychologist form a beneficial therapy team.

With all these avenues of help to choose from, it is important for the survivor to remember that she has the right to shop for the right counseling. Survivors typically do not feel that they have the right to make any demands. But they have, and must assert, the right to find someone they can trust.

Rita, the young woman whose story we have followed in the past few chapters, says this:

The person seeking help should be honest with her counselor about her Christian convictions, not being afraid to tell where she stands. The counselor will respect that position. I couldn't have talked with my pastor—I still couldn't. I think God puts people (like those at the Sexual Assault Center) at his disposal for his purposes. But certainly the abuse survivor has the right to a counselor she feels comfortable with.

What Are Indicators That You Should Seek Psychiatric Help?
According to Dr. J. Ernest Runions, himself a Christian psychiatrist, psychiatric intervention is needed when an individual is characterized by:
1. Intense anxiety, either generalized or focused (phobias, obsessions, etc.)
2. Depression or anxiety of crippling intensity—preventing the person from coping with normal life
3. Any of the above when coupled with physical symptoms
4. Feelings of unreality, of losing a grip on reality
   Psychiatric care combines counseling and medication. Modern psychiatric medication can be a major contributor to restored health.[2]

The Need for Hope

Most important of all, a counselor, whether as a friend and confidante or as a professional therapist, can offer to the abuse survivor what she most needs: hope. Hope that her past need not ruin the rest of her life. Hope that she can break the chains of abuse and walk freely in the present. Hope that the cycle of pain need not be repeated in another generation.

How much counseling will be needed?

Again, this depends on the complexity of one's defense mechanisms in conjunction with the past circumstances. Many people simply refuse to engage in the therapeutic process. They want a sympathetic ear, but they don't want to do any work. The rule of thumb for getting counsel is, "When you're stuck, get help." To evaluate therapy, ask, "Have I grown? Have I made progress in the last three months?" If there is no progress (if you're stuck again), either you are not cooperating significantly or your counselor doesn't have the ability to move you along.

While it is true that some survivors find healing without professional counseling (as Kathy did through her study of Scripture and the support of her prayer partner—and also because of her knowledge as a psychiatric nurse), many will need help at some point in life. The three critical times in the life of a sexual abuse survivor when counseling is most needed are: 1) immediately after the abuse events; 2) at the time of marriage; and 3) when her own children near the age at which she experienced abuse.

For most survivors, the therapeutic process is painful because the past one would like to forget must be confronted and claimed.

> I do want to explore my past, but oh, it hurts so much! I will continue with my Christian counselor . . . I know he cares about me. I cannot deal with this painful issue with someone who just doesn't care.

Abuse survivors have to get back in touch with anesthetized emotions, often reliving the experiences of the past in order to bring healing to the scarred places in their lives. The long-term result of good counseling is that the child sexual abuse is put in place: it happened, it is over, it is healed, and it ceases to be a central (even though hidden) focus. When a person can relate comfortably to the present without having the past throw up its dark shadow, when she no longer feels like a victim but can grow and expand as a normal human being (with both negative and positive emotions), when she's glad that she's a woman, when she can eagerly embrace the gift of each day and turn her face toward the radiant light of Christ, she has been helped to step out of the confining, crippling effects of a sexually-abused past. At last, she can get on with life.

That is help worth finding from whatever source available.

Something You Can Do Right Now

If you are an abuse survivor, you may feel very alone in the healing process. Think of the most loving person you know. Take a few moments (now or over a period of days) and read the following prayer as though it came from that loving person's heart and mouth.

My Lord Jesus,
You were wounded for each one of us.
May the blood from your wounds be poured
like a healing ointment into the wounds
of this person I love.
May this person experience cleansing, release, freedom from
bondage, great new life—and finally joy!
I have great faith that you will answer this prayer
because I know that it is your deepest desire.
I love you, wounded Healer.
Be health now for my friend.
In Christ's name, Amen.

If you are a friend or helper to an abuse survivor, you may pray this prayer for the person for whom you care.

15

Turning Wounds into Ministry

Kathy's Story:

It has been several years now since that day when I received—and gave—forgiveness. It is a long time since I first heard those whispered words, "Be still and know that I am God." Now I know that he is God, *my God.*

That day was a starting point, the beginning of freedom from the prison of anger and hate and guilt in which I had lived. The years since then have been years of growth. As I have studied the Word of God I have come to know my God, and in knowing him I can see the positive—yes, even know the reason why he allowed me the pain of this childhood experience.

My times of study became daily appointments with God when God met with me by his Spirit and revealed to me his truth. Through the Scriptures, I have learned that my God is omniscient: he knows all

(Psalm 139:1–6); he knew all about what happened to me and he knew how I felt. I saw that my God is omnipotent: he possesses all power (Job 42:2); he could have prevented what happened to me, but he didn't. Could there be a purpose? I was beginning to see. My God is omnipresent: he is everywhere (Proverbs 15:3); he saw the evil; he was there with me, yet he allowed it to happen. I also learned that my God is incomprehensible, beyond the understanding of man (Isaiah 55:8–9). We may not always understand the purpose of the tragedies in our lives, but he does, because he sees everything—from beginning to end.

I also came to see that my God is a God of love (1 John 4:8). A God of love who allows this to happen to a little child? Oh, yes. I can see the depth of his love for me. I can see the price he paid for my sin. And I also see the price he paid for the sins of the one who sinned against me. I learned, too, that my God is holy, righteous, just. He is merciful—an actively compassionate being. My God is long-suffering. My God is wise and good. My God is faithful. And yes, my God is wrathful. There is within God a hatred for all that is unrighteous.

But perhaps most important to me was the truth that God is sovereign. What does that mean? It means that God is totally, supremely, and pre-eminently over all his creation (Daniel 4:35). In times of personal tragedy, we cannot say to God, "What have you done?" He is God and we are his creation. We don't have the right to question those things which he has allowed. I believe that God was and is totally, supremely, and pre-eminently over my life and over your life as well (Isaiah 45:5–7). If we know and accept God as being sovereign, we know that all situations are filtered through his fingers of love. Absolutely nothing can touch us unless God allows it (Romans 8:28).

Recently, I found myself thrown into the company of my abuser through family circumstance. While I cannot say he will ever be my favorite person, I can say with great joy that I felt no fear, no hatred, no anger. He, the person who shadowed my life for so long, has absolutely no power over me any more. I am free!

What about regrets? I have none. I have seen that the abuse I experienced was allowed by a sovereign God for purposes of his own, purposes greater than I could have formed for myself. Only recently,

I have found the answer to my lifelong question, "Why?"

You may not all find the answers to your "why's?" I remember Dr. Helen Roseveare telling the story of how she was beaten and brutally raped by rebel soldiers. God spoke to her at that time and asked simply, "Will you trust me, even if I never tell you why?" Sometimes we must simply affirm that kind of trust.

But I did find an answer to my "Why?" and I found it, as I have found most of the important discoveries of my new life, in Scripture. In Isaiah 61, the prophet describes the ministry of reconciliation which would be exercised by the Lord Jesus in his earthly ministry:

> The Spirit of the Sovereign Lord is on me,
> because the Lord has anointed me
> to preach good news to the poor.
> He has sent me to bind up the brokenhearted,
> to proclaim freedom for the captives
> and release for the prisoners . . .
> to comfort all who mourn,
> and provide for those who grieve in Zion—
> to bestow on them a crown of beauty
> instead of ashes,
> the oil of gladness
> instead of mourning,
> and a garment of praise
> instead of a spirit of despair.
> They will be called oaks of righteousness,
> a planting of the Lord
> for the display of his splendor.
> (Isaiah 61:1–3, NIV)

As a child of God, I have been given this ministry as well. It is my joy to bring hope to others who are still imprisoned by their pasts. It is my privilege to live as evidence that God is able to "make all things new" in the life of one who trusts him. The purpose of all this? "The display of God's splendor"—in my life, and in the lives of all those he touches and heals.

169

* ❉ *

As Kathy tells this last segment of her ongoing story, there is joy in her voice. She has been set free from her past. She has been cleansed of its defilement. And she is being used as an instrument of God's grace in the lives of others. For just such a conclusion, our Voices yearn:

> I wish you could tell me about a book where I could find stories of abuse survivors like myself who are living victorious and fruitful lives.

* ❉ *

> Is there any hope that God could use me? I have such a struggle to feel "fit for the Master's use."

The joyful truth is that God is able not only to heal, but also to release the abuse survivor into fruitful, effective living. The circle of ministry may be the family, or the workplace, or the local church fellowship. Some will feel a special urgency to reach out to others who, like themselves, have lived under the long shadow of sexual abuse. Others will be eager to forget that past completely and minister Christ's love by being an effective mother, a good wife, a caring colleague.

The whole range of ministry—the opportunity to use personal spiritual gifts—lies open before the person who has experienced, and is experiencing, healing. "You were washed, you were sanctified, you were justified in the name of the Lord Jesus Christ and by the Spirit of our God" (1 Corinthians 6:11, NIV). Cleansed. Set apart for service. Made perfectly right in God's eyes. The hymn-writer puts it this way:

> Ransomed, healed, restored, forgiven,
> Who like me his praise shall sing?[1]

Spheres of Ministry

I like to think of spheres of ministry as being like concentric circles. The bull's-eye or center circle is ministry to those closest to us: our families. The next circle is ministry within our local church fellowship

170

(a Sunday School class that needs a teacher? a visiting program to a nursing home that needs a volunteer?). The third circle is ministry within our community. I often ask Jesus the same question as the young lawyer in Luke 10:29, although in a different tone, "Lord, who is my neighbor?" I have learned that *my neighbor is the person near me right now whose needs I am able to meet.*

Women have often told me of their desire to minister. But somehow, they often think of it as something they have to do "out there." Some sigh, "I think I was made to reach a bigger audience than this." With a shrug, they indicate the mini-audience of family or classroom or close friends. I think of the scriptural principle: faithful in little, ruler over much. Meeting family needs, listening and being a friend, loving the unlovely and forgotten: these are significant ministries in God's sight.

Caring for Others Who Have Been Abused

Those who have experienced child abuse are very often deeply empathetic and compassionate toward suffering children and adults with similar experiences. Ministering from the healing of God is often a very natural extension of the grace that has been received. Here are some of the ministry fronts where people who have experienced substantial healing can take their places.

1. *Person-to-Person Sharing the Good News of Healing:* As the extent of the problem of child abuse becomes generally known, we must realize that there are simply not enough professional or pastoral counselors to go around. People will have to minister to each other, sharing with the next person the comfort they have received in their distress. As one person tells his/her story, others begin to admit their needs in the same area, and healing is shared.

2. *Heightening Awareness in the Church:* People who have experienced child abuse may become the conscience of the church. Setting up a committee to find out how and where the church should minister to children and adults in the area of abuse would be a starting point. People with the gift of administration are needed here to form structures where, within a context of Christian love and care and a biblical view

of man and God, people can find help. People in pastoral ministries need to be trained in detecting and helping people confront the problem of abuse. Support groups for survivors could be set up. The church ministry should not overlook the trauma of the mother in many incestuous situations, and the need of the perpetrator to take responsibility for his sin and to seek to make amends.

3. *Promoting Awareness in Legislatures:* Much needs to be done to make lawmakers aware of the long-term effects of child abuse. A beginning has been made here, but legislators still seem to draw back from creating laws with real bite—laws which would make the punishment commensurate with the damage inflicted by the crime. There needs to be careful thought as to how society can best respond to the problem of violence—and especially sexual violence—against children. Christians who have been wounded and healed may be the best spokespersons for the cause of justice in this neglected area.

A Word of Caution
But as abuse survivors seek to turn their woundedness into hope and healing for others, there are several cautions to be kept in mind. First of all, survivors should not try to minister in this area too soon. They will feel passion and compassion, but may not be emotionally strong enough to cope with the added pressure of carrying others' burdens until they have had some experience of living in the light.

For many, initial ministry might be simply sharing in the ordinary church context, rebuilding relationships at home or in the workplace, growing in understanding of God and self. In considering any kind of ministry opportunity, survivors need to think through some of these questions:

—Will this kind of ministry enhance or imperil the emotional stability I have now achieved, either through reopening painful areas of memory, or through physical and/or mental pressure?
—Will this kind of ministry enhance or imperil the gains that I have made in building better relationships with others? Will it have a positive or negative impact on my family life?
—Will this kind of ministry enhance or imperil the prayer life that

I have established as a lifeline? Will there still be time for Bible study/reading and for prayer, or will there be the danger of time constraints cutting me off from the sustenance needed for vital Christian living?

More than once I have pondered an urgent request for help from some group or another, recognizing the dilemma faced by "The Other Wise Man" in Henry Van Dyke's great story. Considering whether he should use his last gem to ransom a slave girl or whether he should save it to give to the long-sought King, Artaban wonders, "Was it his great opportunity or his last temptation?"[2]

We have to learn to distinguish between opportunity and temptation. I have been much encouraged by Colleen Townsend Evans in this regard. She teaches that there are seasons in our lives, and that each season has its opportunities and its limitations. "What might be a suitable ministry for one season might be totally unsuitable for another," she reminds women, recalling her own over-extension as a young mother and minister's wife. "I realize now I was trying to do too much, taking on ministries suitable for a later season too soon, and so I was fatigued and off-balance."[3]

There is yet another caution to be heeded before we hurry into ministry. This warning is sounded by the writer of Hebrews: "See to it . . . that no bitter root grows up to cause trouble and defile many" (Hebrews 12:15, NIV). If there is a sliver of unforgiveness left in our hearts, a residual anger that still smolders, the "root of bitterness" is likely to hinder our ministry. We have, perhaps, all heard people speaking about a painful past in such a way that the message seems to be a kind of revenge. Public statements can become a way to strike back at a family that failed to protect, or a church that failed to respond. A truly healing ministry cannot be exercised except by those whose wounded hearts have known the healing oil of the Spirit of God.

Whom Shall I tell? How Much Shall I Tell?
I have talked about the importance of claiming the pain-filled past in words—either orally or through a journal. But one must be careful about "going public" with the story of a painful or sordid past. (You

will notice that those Voices who have spoken in this book have been carefully made anonymous—for reasons that might be important to all survivors). Some of the questions that need to be answered before a story is told beyond the person-to-person sharing are these:

—Who may be hurt if I tell this story now? What about my parents? my brothers and sisters? my children? Is the possibility of deep hurt within my inner family circle worth the potential ministry?
—Does my husband feel fully comfortable with my declaration of this as my past, or would he be more comfortable if I were to keep this a private matter? Since misunderstanding here will be reflected in your total relationship, don't be too quick to assume that because you feel healed of the past, your husband has fully dealt with his anger and pain.
—How fully am I healed? If there is still healing to be done, it might be better to "be still and know . . . God" for a while longer.

Remembering that the first task of life is to build healthy and healing relationships in our own personal circles of love, the survivor can ask simply, "Dear Lord, what ministry do you wish to flow from my healed wounds? As life has flowed to me from the healed wounds of my Savior, so may hope flow to others from my own cleansed and healed wounds."

We shouldn't hurry or feel pressured into a ministry or activity by some kind of false guilt. Rather, we should move steadily, quietly in the easy yoke into which our Lord invites us (Matthew 11:28–29). May we all find opportunity to serve our Lord, our brothers and sisters, and those around us who do not yet know Christ's healing touch.

There is one last story I want to share with you. I've saved it for the last. To tell it, let me introduce another friend.

Margaret

Margaret is the kind of woman you would like to know: attractive, poised, articulate. In her work overseas, she communicates in three languages, works comfortably with government officials or tribal leaders, and has a first-hand knowledge of international affairs. She is a grandmother many times over and is concerned with the growing families of her children. She has been involved in relief efforts for people displaced by warfare. Whether teaching in a tribal village or a graduate program in a university, she is clearly a person who knows and uses her gifts. Margaret is the epitome of fruitful, meaningful womanhood, and she shares her story here as a sign of hope for abuse survivors.

16

Behold, I Make All Things New

Margaret's Story:

I was about five when my father first began to fondle me. When he began to have sex with my older sister when she was nine, I was terrified that it would happen to me — which, of course, it did.

From the time I was nine until I was thirteen, my father used me as a sexual partner. I thought that if my sister and I kept him satisfied, perhaps he would not bother our younger sisters. But in time he got to them as well.

My parents quarreled a great deal, and my mother and all of us children were battered and bruised in my father's violent outbursts. Much as we feared his anger when he was drunk, we feared even more his fury when, at some small provocation, he flared into rage and beat us when he was sober.

His violence was backed up with threats of using a revolver he had come to own during a period as a police officer. We knew it was there and never doubted that he might use it. One terrible night he did, shooting my mother through the abdomen and very nearly killing her. He was arrested for attempted murder, and my mother was taken by ambulance to the hospital.

For many weeks we did not hear from either of our parents. My older sister and I, then fourteen and thirteen, cared for the four younger children the best we could, subsisting through a long summer on our twenty-acre farm. When my mother finally recovered sufficiently to make some decisions, she worked out a plea-bargaining deal whereby she would not press criminal charges. My father, in return for this, was to give her custody of the children and make support payments.

My father was released from jail and immediately married a woman with whom he had been unfaithful to my mother—a woman whose daughters he would subsequently abuse.

My mother and we six children moved to another part of the state to pick up the pieces of our lives. My mother worked full time to care for the family, my father never contributing anything at all to our support. She came home day after day, tired to the bone. I realize now how frayed she must have felt, but no matter how hard my sisters and brother and I tried to please her—with an especially good meal or a freshly cleaned house—she seemed only aware of the one thing left undone. She was never appreciative and always critical, leaving me feeling very unsure of myself throughout my adult life.

My sister escaped the family situation by finding another home in which to live while she went to high school. But I stayed on with mother, caring for my younger brother and sisters, leaving time for only the academic aspect of school.

We had begun to attend church when we moved. At first, my mother felt too keenly the stigma of her divorce (in those days a real scandal) and did not come with us. Later she began to enter into the life of the church. Our family's past was known, however, and I can recall that some families actually withdrew their children from the youth choir when I joined. In general, though, we found more acceptance in the church than anywhere else in that town.

The one place where I succeeded was school. My grades were good, despite frequent absenteeism to help care for children at home. I set myself a liberation timeline: after graduation from high school, I decided firmly, I would leave home and go to college. I had, from very early childhood, been working out a plan whereby my life could be different from my parents' and the life of my children different from my own abused and ashamed childhood.

I remember one high school English teacher in particular who treated me with respect and made me feel that I was, in some way, worthwhile. I especially remember her inviting me to her home — a very important affirmation to me.

After two years of college, I married a boy I had met while I was in high school and who, despite his parents' objections, loved me. The summer we were married, while he was a student minister, we had a definite conversion experience in which we came to understand the meaning of the death of Christ on our behalf and claimed his death as the basis of our salvation.

Although we had been good "church kids," we had not previously had the experience of the indwelling Christ. This new faith dynamic set us alight. We met with other Christians for fellowship, studied the Bible, and prayed with a new sense of relatedness to God. Gradually, while studying at a Christian college, we became aware of a desire to commit ourselves to foreign missions.

Meanwhile, our family began to arrive. Throughout my first pregnancy I struggled with excessive nausea which I now attribute to anxiety about what kind of mother I would be. But I had from early childhood thought through, "When I am a mother, I will do . . ." and, "I won't ever . . ."

I was determined to break the cycle of abuse, and by God's grace, I have. With a large family all grown, all married, all loving and serving God, I can reassure other anxious-hearted abuse survivors that *the cycle can be broken*. The pain does not have to be passed on.

Raising children in another culture has been a rugged, rich, and rewarding experience, despite the distance from medical and educational facilities.

I have experienced substantial healing, but it has not been without pain. I have learned that even when I thought I had dealt with the past, there are times when I must offer forgiveness again. Memories arise unbidden and must be dealt with. "How often should I forgive my brother?" Peter asked Jesus. In Jesus' answer, "Seventy times seven." I have heard this: forgiveness must be offered as many times as the hurtful memory arises.

My constant need for affirmation has sometimes been difficult within our marriage. My husband, while strongly supportive and loving, is not tremendously verbal about it. We have needed help and counseling to get through some hard places. But through it all, my husband has been my therapist, and Jesus, my healer.

I suspect the process of such healing may last the rest of my life. But I can truly say that *I am being healed.*

* * *

Margaret's story affirms that an abusive past need not be a burden, coloring the present, shadowing the future. There is much need for hope and healing in the lives of child sexual abuse victims and abusers—the kind of hope Christ can give; healing so that the cycle of abuse will not be repeated in the lives of children or others the abuse survivor loves. The chains of the past *can* be broken. The abuse survivor can walk freely into the future—with God's help.

For Kathy, the real cleansing of her pain-filled past came with the recognition of the sovereign power and purposes of her God. It was through her understanding of his sovereignty, as portrayed in the Scriptures—his ability to bring good out of evil—that she came to a place of rest.

Margaret also recognized God's sovereign power in her life—power that continues to heal the scars. She also recalls many circumstances where helpers were essential in her healing process (the high school teacher who showed a special interest, marriage counselors).

Many of our Voices speak of the importance of Christian community in fostering healing and building healthy relationships with the survivor and abuser. We, as Christ's church, need to realize that adult survivors and child abusers *do* need our support—as a group, as families, and as individuals.

I urge you to get involved. There are many organizations that need assistance in fighting the evil of child sexual abuse—government or-

ganizations, church programs, counseling programs, volunteer programs. Or you could start your own. What about your neighbors? the
calloused man, the shy woman, the fearful child down the block who
desperately needs a friend? They all need someone to listen, hold them
accountable, and with the Spirit's help, open that door of healing in
their damaged souls.

God calls us all—each with varied talents and resources—to act as
instruments of his grace in the lives of others. As a community of
caring, concerned Christians, we have a responsibility to minister to
each other. And as Christ's healing flows through you and cleanses
your wounds, so let it flow through you to others who are hurting.
For all those who are wounded, that is indeed a tremendous hope for
healing.

Kathy's Prayer

Father, our hearts well up within us as we thank you and praise you for being God.

We thank you and praise you that there is hope, there is joy, there is peace, and there is love found in you. We thank you, Father, that you can take the wounds and the brokenness of our lives and change them and transform them to your honor and to your glory.

Father, you more than anybody else, know the hurts that lie within our hearts. By your Holy Spirit, gently and lovingly touch us in the areas where we need your healing ministry. Cause us to face those things that torment us—not run away and hide. Encourage us to lay them open before you and to be willing to give you a chance to heal our wounded selves. We praise and thank you for your willingness to do this.

Through Jesus our Lord, Amen.

Appendix: Where Do We Go From Here?

Moving from ignorance or denial to determined action is a kind of "pilgrim's progress" for each of us (see Appendix Figure). Many who have read this book will be asking: "What can I do?" The list of ideas below can help you find your own personal starting point in confronting and combating the evil of child sexual abuse.

If You Are a Survivor:
1. Work through the self-help sections of this book thoroughly.
2. Find someone to share your story with.
3. Seek counseling. If none is available, contact your minister and ask that the church move to meet this need.
4. Become a member of an abuse survivor's group, or form one with the help of a counselor with some training in this kind of therapy.
5. Begin personal Bible study and prayer.
6. Help one other abuse survivor.

If You Are a Helping Friend:
1. Share this book with your friend or neighbor who has a past history of abuse. Offer to work through it with him/her.
2. See what counseling services are available in your area.
3. Take some basic sexual assault counseling training if such is available in your area.
4. Urge your church, women's group, and Christian Education committee to plan programs to help survivors.

If You Are a Church Leader:
1. Become thoroughly informed about child sexual abuse, particularly within the Christian community.
2. Assess the needs of your congregation and community with regard to both prevention and therapy.
3. Educate your Christian Education personnel (Sunday School teachers and youth workers) in the detection and counseling of children who have been sexually (or otherwise) abused.
4. Work with local agencies such as Sexual Assault Centers to develop awareness of the problem within your congregation and community.
5. Assess the counseling resources of your church and community. Could you provide better services with better training? How could that be arranged?
6. Extend your concern to other areas of family violence.
7. Consider the ways that theological assumptions are used to justify/cover up child sexual abuse. What can you do in teaching/preaching/family life support programs to correct misapprehensions about male dominance exercised through power within the family?
8. Form a committee including one or more abuse survivors to inform the church about this growing problem. Suggest strategies for meeting the needs of family members who are involved in some way with child sexual abuse. Include both perpetrator and victims.

For More Information, Contact:

Clearinghouse on Child Abuse and Neglect Information
P.O. Box 1182
Washington, D.C. 20013
(301) 251-5157

National Clearinghouse on Family Violence
Brooke Claxton Building, Ninth Floor
Health and Welfare Canada
Ottawa, Ontario K1A 1B5 Canada

Appendix Figure. The "pilgrim's progress" to determined action

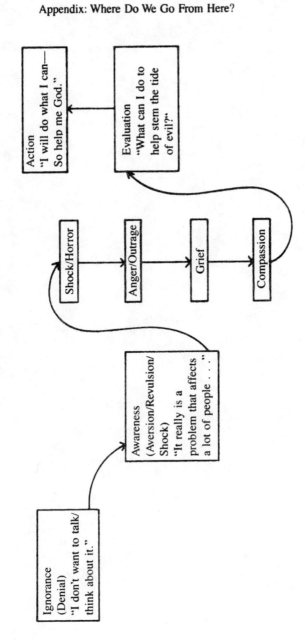

187

Notes

1/The Nature of Child Sexual Abuse

1. Zaphiris, Alexander G. *Methods and Skills for a Differential Assessment and Treatment in Incest, Sexual Abuse and Sexual Exploitation of Children* (Denver: The American Humane Association, 1983), p. 3.
2. Butler, Sandra. *Conspiracy of Silence: The Trauma of Incest* (San Francisco: New Glide Publications, 1978), p. 31.
3. Zaphiris, *Methods and Skills*, p. 3.
4. Finkelhor, David. *Sexually Victimized Children* (New York: The Free Press, a division of MacMillan Company, 1979), pp. 87, 132.
   Russell, Diana. "The Incidence and Prevalence of Intrafamilial and Extrafamilial Sexual Abuse of Female Children," *Child Abuse and Neglect*, 7 (1983), p. 137.
5. Russell, D., p. 137.
6. Russell, Alene Bycer and Cynthia Mohr Trainor, *Trends in Child Abuse and Neglect: A National Perspective* (Denver: The American Humane Association, Children's Division, 1984), p. 137.
7. Butman, Richard E. "Hidden Victims: The Facts about Incest," *HIS Magazine*, April 1983.

2/The Physical and Emotional Aftermath

1. Forward, Susan and Craig Buck. *Betrayal of Innocence: Incest and Its Devastation* (New York: Penguin Books, 1978), p. 20.

189

Child Sexual Abuse: A Hope for Healing

2. Armstrong, Louise. *Kiss Daddy Goodnight: A Speak-Out on Incest* (New York: Hathorne Books, Inc., 1978), p. 67.
3. Rush, Florence. *The Best Kept Secret: Sexual Abuse of Children* (Englewood Cliffs, NJ: Prentice-Hall, Inc., 1980), p. 195.
4. Meiselman, Karin C. *Incest: A Psychological Study of Causes and Effects with Treatment Recommendations* (San Francisco: Jossey-Bass, Inc., 1978), p. 188.
5. Tsai, Mavis and Nathaniel N. Wagner. "Therapy Groups for Women Sexually Molested as Children," *Archives of Sexual Behavior,* 7, #5, 1958.
6. Steele, Brandt F. and Helen Alexander. "Long-term Effects of Sexual Abuse in Childhood," in Mrazek, Patricia Beezley and C. Henry Kempe, *Sexually Abused Children and Their Families* (New York: Pergamon Press, 1981), pp. 223-233.
7. Forward and Buck, p. 20.
8. Meiselman, p. 198.
9. Siemers, Mary Ellen. "Treatment Methods for Adult Female Survivors of Incest: A Review of the Literature," unpublished master's thesis, University of Wisconsin, May 1986, pp. 11-13.
10. Green, Holly Wagner. *Turning Fear to Hope* (Nashville: Thomas Nelson Publishers, 1984), p. 78.
11. Allen, Charlotte Vale. *Daddy's Girl* (Toronto: McClelland and Stewart, 1980), p. 92.

3/Behavioral and Relational Problems
1. Freud, Anna. "A Psychoanalyst's View of Sexual Abuse by Parents" in *Sexually Abused Children and Their Families* by Patricia Beezley Mrazek and C. Henry Kempe (New York: Pergamon Press, 1981), pp. 33-34.
2. Finkelhor, Chapter seven.
3. Meiselman, p. 186.
4. Cohen, Tamar. "The Incestuous Family Revisited," *Social Casework: The Journal of Contemporary Social Work,* March 1983, p. 158.
5. Steele and Alexander, p. 233.
6. Densen-Gerber, Judianne. "Incest as a Causative Factor in Anti-Social Behavior: An Exploratory Study" in *Child Abuse: Where Do We Go From Here?*, conference proceedings, Children's Memorial Hospital National Medical Center, February 18-20, 1977, pp. 83-88.
7. Meiselman, p. 230.
8. Forward and Buck, p. 22.
9. Tsai and Wagner, p. 423.
10. Meiselman, p. 215.
11. Justice, Blair and Rita Justice. *The Broken Taboo: Sex in the Family* (New York: Human Sciences Press, 1979), p. 187.
12. Meiselman, p. 245.
13. Tsai and Wagner, p. 424.

4/The Shadowed Spirit
1. Colson, Charles. *Who Speaks for God?* (Westchester, IL: Crossway Books, 1985), p. 31.
2. Forward and Buck, p. 23.
3. Schaeffer, Francis. *The God Who Is There* (Downers Grove, IL: InterVarsity Press, 1968), p. 102.
4. White, John. *Masks of Melancholy* (Downers Grove, IL: InterVarsity Press, 1982), p. 202.
5. Meiselman, p. 347.

Notes

5/Claiming the Past
1. Allen.
2. Ricks, Chip. Preface to *Carol's Story* (Carol Stream, IL: Tyndale House Publishers, 1981).
3. Klug, Ron. "Looking Backward" in *How to Keep a Spiritual Journal* (Nashville: Thomas Nelson Publishers, 1984).
4. Tavris, Carol. *Anger: The Misunderstood Emotion* (New York: Simon and Schuster, 1982), p. 23.
5. Tavris, p. 23.
6. Lake, Frank. *Tight Corners in Pastoral Counseling* (Darton, Longman, and Todd, 1981), p. 137.

6/The Freedom of Forgiveness
1. Smedes, Lewis B. *How Can It Be All Right When Everything Is All Wrong?* (San Francisco: Harper & Row, Inc., 1982), p. 33.
2. Dickens, Charles. *Great Expectations*.
3. *Webster's New Twentieth Century Dictionary*, definition 1.
4. *Webster's*, definition 2.
5. ten Boom, Corrie. *The Hiding Place* (Old Tappan, NJ: Fleming H. Revell, 1971), p. 215.

7/The Journey Toward Healing
1. Forward and Buck, p. 166.
2. Peck, M. Scott. *The Road Less Traveled* (New York: Simon and Schuster, 1978) p. 55.
3. White, John, p. 202.
4. Mother Theresa. *Words to Love By . . .* (Notre Dame: Ave Maria Press, 1983), p. 40.

8/Seeing God as He Really Is
1. Hester, Richard L. *Family Stories as Bearers of the Family's Theology.* Unpublished manuscript, 1983, pp. 88-90.
2. Tozer, A. W. *The Knowledge of the Holy* (New York: Harper & Row, Inc., 1961), p. 117.

10/Understanding the Abuser
1. Summit, Roland. "Typical Characteristics of Father-Daughter Incest: A Guide for Investigation." Unpublished paper, pp. 18-19.
2. Justice and Justice, *The Broken Taboo*, p. 69.
3. Butman, p. 21.
4. Groth, A. Nicholas and William F. Hobson and Thomas S. Gary. "The Child Molester: Clinical Observation," in *Social Work and Child Sexual Abuse*, ed. Jon R. Conte and David A. Shore, 1982, pp. 129-144.
5. Badgley, Robin, et al. *Sexual Offenses Against Children in Canada* (Ottawa: Canadian Government Publishing Centre, 1984).
6. Scott, David Alexander. *Pornography: Its Effects on the Family, Community and Culture* (Guild of Family Protection Institute, 1984), p. 13.
7. Armstrong, p. 235.
8. Summit, p. 13.
9. Summit, p. 15.
10. Meiselman, p. 180.
11. Monfalcone, Wesley R. *Coping with Abuse in the Family* (Philadelphia: The Westminster Press, 1980), pp. 72-75.
12. Summit, p. 16.

13. O'Brien, Shirley. *Child Pornography* (Dubuque, IA: Kendall/Hunt Publishing, 1983), p. 82.
14. Armstrong, p. 234.
15. Groth, Nicholas. *Men Who Rape: The Psychology of the Offender* (New York: Plenum Publishing Corp., 1979).
16. Badgley.
17. Scott, p. 13.
18. Badgley.
19. Scott, p. 7.
20. Scott, p. 9.
21. Zaphiris, Alexander G. "Father-Daughter Incest" in *Sexual Abuse of Children: Implications for Treatment* (Colorado: Child Protection Division, 1983), p. 90.

11/Portrait of an Abuser
1. Justice and Justice, *The Broken Taboo*, p. 244.

12/The Mother of the Abused
1. O'Brien, Shirley. *We Can! Combat Child Sexual Abuse* (Tucson, AZ: College of Agriculture, University of Arizona, 1982), pp. 27-29.
2. Meiselman, p. 219.
3. Armstrong, p. 239.
4. Nanaimo Rape Assault Centre. "Realities of Child Sexual Abuse," a noncopyrighted mimeographed project, pp. 51-52.

13/Renewing Relationships
1. Runions, Dr. J. Ernest, medical director, interview. Coquitlam, B.C.: British Columbia Hospital.
2. Freud, Sigmund. Studies on Hysteria in Rush, Florence, *The Best Kept Secret: Sexual Abuse of Children* (Englewood Cliffs, NJ: Prentice-Hall, Inc., 1980), pp. 80ff.
3. Kinsey, Alfred. From an unpublished manual by Alice Huskey, as quoted in the "Chapel of the Air" broadcast of April 18, 1985, "So Help Us God" by Karen Mains.
4. Smiley, Gene. "Jesus Loves the Little Children, Black and Blue" in *The Sunday School Counselor,* Vol. 44, #9, September 1984, p. 47.
5. Miller, Kathy Collard. *Out of Control! A Christian Parent's Victorious Struggle with Child Abuse* (Waco: Word Books, Inc., 1984).

14/The Helpers
1. Goleman, Daniel. *Vital Lies, Simple Truths: The Psychology of Self-Deception and Shared Illusions* (New York: Simon and Schuster, 1985), p. 153.
2. Runions interview.

15/Turning Wounds Into Ministry
1. Lyte, Henry F. "Praise, My Soul, the King of Heaven" in *Hymns II* (Downers Grove, IL: InterVarsity Press), #9.
2. Van Dyke, Henry. *The Story of the Other Wise Man* (London: Wyvern Books, 1961), p. 90.
3. Evans, Colleen Townsend. Verbal address at the *Women Alive!* conference at the University of Waterloo, April 27, 1984.

Bibliography

Allen, Charlotte Vale. *Daddy's Girl*. Toronto: McClelland and Stewart, 1980.

Armstrong, Louise. *Kiss Daddy Goodnight: A Speak-Out on Incest*. New York: Hathorne Books, Inc., 1978.

Badgley, Robin, et al. *Sexual Offenses Against Children in Canada*. Ottawa: Canadian Government Publishing Centre, 1984.

Butler, Sandra. *Conspiracy of Silence: The Trauma of Incest*. San Francisco: New Glide Publications, 1978.

Butman, Richard E. "Hidden Victims: The Facts about Incest," in *HIS* Magazine, April 1983.

Cohen, Tamar. "The Incestuous Family Revisited." *Social Casework: The Journal of Contemporary Social Work,* March 1983.

Colson, Charles. *Who Speaks for God?* Westchester, IL: Crossway Books, 1985.

Densen-Gerber, Judianne. "Incest as a Causative Factor in Anti-Social Behavior: An Exploratory Study" in *Child Abuse: Where Do We Go From Here?* conference proceedings, Children's Memorial Hospital National Medical Center, February 1977.

Evans, Colleen Townsend. Verbal address at the *Women Alive!* conference at the University of Waterloo, April 27, 1984.

Finkelhor, David. *Sexually Victimized Children*. New York: The Free Press, a division of MacMillan Company, 1979.

Forward, Susan and Craig Buck. *Betrayal of Innocence: Incest and Its Devastation*. New York: Penguin Books, 1978.

193

Child Sexual Abuse: A Hope for Healing

Freud, Anna. "A Psychoanalyst's View of Sexual Abuse by Parents" from *Sexually Abused Children and Their Families* by Patricia Beezley Mrazek and C. Henry Kempe. New York: Pergamon Press, 1981.

Goleman, Daniel. *Vital Lies, Simple Truths: The Psychology of Self-Deception and Shared Illusions*. New York: Simon and Schuster, 1985.

Groth, A. Nicholas. *Men Who Rape: The Psychology of the Offender*. New York: Plenum Publishing Corp., 1979.

Groth, A. Nicholas and William F. Hobson and Thomas S. Gary. "The Child Molester: Clinical Observation," in *Social Work and Child Sexual Abuse*, ed. J.R. Conte and D.A. Shore, 1982.

Green, Holly Wagner. *Turning Fear to Hope*. Nashville: Thomas Nelson Publishers, 1984.

Hester, Richard L. *Family Stories as Bearers of the Family's Theology*. Unpublished manuscript, 1983.

Justice, Blair and Rita Justice. *The Broken Taboo: Sex in the Family*. New York: Human Sciences Press, 1979.

Kinsey, Alfred. In an unpublished manual by Alice Huskey, as quoted in the "Chapel of the Air" broadcast "So Help Us God" on April 18, 1985 by Karen Mains.

Klug, Ron. "Looking Backward" in *How to Keep a Spiritual Journal*. Nashville: Thomas Nelson Publishers, 1984.

Lake, Frank. *Tight Corners in Pastoral Counseling*. Darton, Longman, and Todd, 1981.

Lewis, C.S. *The Problem of Pain*. New York: MacMillan Company, 1962.

Lyte, Henry F. "Praise, My Soul, the King of Heaven" in *Hymns II*. Downers Grove, IL: InterVarsity Press, #9.

Meiselman, Karin C. *Incest: A Psychological Study of Causes and Effects with Treatment Recommendations*. San Francisco: Jossey-Bass, Inc., 1978.

Miller, Kathy Collard. *Out of Control: A Christian Parent's Victorious Struggle with Child Abuse*. Waco: Word Books, Inc., 1984.

Monfalcone, Wesley R. *Coping with Abuse in the Family*. Philadelphia: The Westminster Press, 1980.

Mother Theresa. *Words to Love By* . . . Notre Dame: Ave Maria Press, 1983.

Nanaimo Rape Assault Centre. "Realities of Child Sexual Abuse," a noncopyrighted mimeographed project. Nanaimo Rape Assault Centre.

O'Brien, Shirley. *Child Pornography*. Dubuque, IA: Kendall/Hunt Publishing, 1983.

O'Brien, Shirley. *We Can! Combat Child Sexual Abuse*. Tucson, AZ: College of Agriculture, University of Arizona, 1982.

Peck, M. Scott. *The Road Less Traveled*. New York: Simon and Schuster, 1983.

Ricks, Chip. Preface to *Carol's Story*. Carol Stream, IL: Tyndale House Publishers, 1981.

Runions, Dr. J. Ernest, medical director. Interview. Coquitlam, B.C.: British Columbia Hospital.

Rush, Florence. *The Best Kept Secret: Sexual Abuse of Children*. Englewood Cliffs, NJ: Prentice-Hall, Inc., 1980.

Russell, Alene Bycer and Cynthia Mohr Trainor. *Trends in Child Abuse and Neglect: A National Perspective*. Denver: The American Humane Association, Children's Division, 1984.

Russell, Diana. "The Incidence and Prevalence of Intrafamilial and Extrafamilial Sexual Abuse of Female Children." *Child Abuse and Neglect*, 7, 1983.

Schaeffer, Francis. *The God Who Is There*. Downers Grove, IL: InterVarsity Press, 1968.

Scott, David Alexander. *Pornography: Its Effects on the Family, Community and Culture*. Guild of Family Protection Institute, 1984.

Siemers, Mary Ellen. "Treatment Methods for Adult Female Survivors of Incest: A Review of the Literature." Unpublished master's thesis, University of Wisconsin, May 1986.

Bibliography

Smedes, Lewis B. *How Can It Be All Right When Everything Is All Wrong?* San Francisco: Harper and Row, Inc., 1982.

Smiley, Gene. "Jesus Loves the Little Children, Black and Blue" in *The Sunday School Counselor,* Vol. 44, #9, September 1984.

Steele, Brandt F. and Helen Alexander. "Long-term Effects of Sexual Abuse in Childhood," in Mrazek, Patricia Beezley and C. Henry Kempe, *Sexually Abused Children and Their Families.* New York: Pergamon Press, 1981.

Summit, Roland. "Typical Characteristics of Father-Daughter Incest: A Guide for Investigation." Unpublished paper.

Tavris, Carol. *Anger: The Misunderstood Emotion.* New York: Simon and Schuster, 1982.

ten Boom, Corrie. *The Hiding Place.* Old Tappan, NJ: Fleming H. Revell Company, 1971.

Tozer, A.W. *The Knowledge of the Holy.* New York: Harper & Row, Inc., 1961.

Tsai, Mavis and Nathaniel N. Wagner. "Therapy Groups for Women Sexually Molested as Children." *Archives of Sexual Behavior,* 7, #5, 1958.

Van Dyke, Henry. *The Story of the Other Wise Man.* London: Wyvern Books, 1961.

Webster's New Twentieth Century Dictionary.

White, John. *Masks of Melancholy.* Downers Grove, IL: InterVarsity Press, 1982.

Zaphiris, Alexander G. "Father-Daughter Incest" in *Sexual Abuse of Children: Implications for Treatment.* Colorado: Child Protection Division, 1983.

Zaphiris, Alexander G. *Methods and Skills for a Differential Assessment and Treatment in Incest, Sexual Abuse and Sexual Exploitation of Children.* Denver: The American Humane Association, 1983.

Index

197